A DISTANCE TRAVELED

IN THE LIGHT OF DISTANT SUNS

POEMS, PROSE

& OTHER TREASURES

BY ROBERT BUCKNER

A Distance Traveled
In The Light Of Distant Suns

Acknowledgements:

Andy Buckner - for the typing of my hand written journal.

Brian Buckner - for lending an ear when I needed to share.

David Buckner - for thoughts, suggestions and encouragement.

S. B. and A. B. for proofing and suggested edits.

And to readers of this book –
May the time spent with this book be a good distance traveled.
My heart is filled with gratitude for the encouragement of all who
believed in me. Encouragement is the light that kept me going;
sometimes late into the night, as I labored through the many hours
it takes to bring a book to print.

Robert (Bob) Buckner
Creative Dreamings Press
www.creativedreamings.com

DEDICATION

To Barb and our three sons, to family, friends and distances traveled. To all who have been a part of my life – through the years or in a brief moments passing – for the gift of life we have shared and of time, precious to us all.

CONTENTS

PREFACE

I was searching the archives of my work stored in an old oak cabinet in the hopes of finding material for use in this book. I came across the following lines, handwritten on a single sheet of paper.

How often I think of the many people who have been a light in my life. My soul is filled with the light of love because of their loving care, concern and friendship. Someday, I will write about them. Well, perhaps this is the day if I continue to endure and carry this process onto fruition.

Those few lines written years before are the essence of what this book is about.

I was never good at English and for the most part didn't care much for writing. In my senior year of high school I was introduced to the works of Shakespeare in English class. I was intrigued, not so much by the writing and plays of Shakespeare but by the Globe Theatre where the works of Shakespeare came to life. I decided to build a balsa wood and cardboard model of the Globe Theatre. I combed the card catalogues and bookshelves of the James J. Hill Reference Library in downtown Saint Paul, Minnesota in search of more information. After several hours of searching I found what I needed. I made some sketches, jotted some notes and Xeroxed several pages from a few books I found.

A few weeks later and after hours of work, I brought my finished model of the Globe Theatre to school and presented it to Mr. Endres and the class. Several days later Mr. Endres informed me that because of my initiative, research and work on the model I would receive an "A" for the quarter. The one and only "A" I ever received in an English class.

At the time I was halfway through my senior year of high school, still trying to figure out what to do about college and a career. Thinking about my experience working on the Globe Theatre model I decided that I might enjoy work in the field of art and design.

I collected some drawings I had saved and supplemented what I had with a few new drawings and hastily put together a portfolio within in a few weeks' time. I took it to Mr. Franz, a teacher who I had in a prior year's religion class and whose art I had seen and appreciated. After a quick look at my work he suggested that it might be better if I pursued studies in something other than art. Showing me the more skilled and developed work of other students he informed me that work as an artist was difficult and competitive. It was not the response I had hoped to hear; however it was truthful and honest. Stubborn and determined, I continued on to Art College and never looked back, for art and design was and is my passion.

Somehow, along life's way, I came to realize that writing was in many ways not much different than the art I so enjoyed. Writing, like art, is a creative process that communicates feelings, thoughts and ideas.

And so it was that I came to enjoy the process and the challenge of writing. I acknowledge the critiques of my writing and of my art through the years. The honest assessments and suggestions of others have helped me grow as an artist, a writer and a person.

INTRODUCTION

art [ahrt] *noun* - The love of the viewer, the artist, plying the dark and light, transforming canvas, film, screen or
space, through shape, color and light, into wonder and life.

poetry [poh-i-tree] *noun* - The love of the reader, the
writer, plying the dark and light, transforming words on
paper, into wonder and life. The music of words, written
and spoken.

prose [prohz] *noun* - The love of the listener, the reader, the storyteller, plying the dark and light, transforming
the ordinary of our days, into wonder and life.

I begin the introduction of this book with definitions of art, poetry and prose that are meaningful to me and I believe relative to the selected works within the pages of this book. Each definition begins with the phrasing, "The love of..." referencing not only the author or the artist but the reader and the viewer as well. Without the reader, the viewer, the work of an author or artist never resolves, never transforms.

One of the last definitions of an "artist" to be found in most dictionaries references "persons whose work exhibits exceptional skill." While the definition is listed last, in my view it is by no means the least. The skill, expertise, and dedication of our work make a difference in the lives of others. And so the work we do, whether or not we consider ourselves as "artists" does touch hearts, souls and the lives of others in ways we may not know or comprehend.

I learned at an early age, the empowering transformation of thought in the movement of pencil and crayon on paper. Those early works were often saved and treasured by those I respected and loved, and most especially by my mother. In time, with encouragement, hard work and persistence, art became an important and treasured part of my life.

Later in my career working with clients, I was often asked to write, in addition to my work as an artist. While I enjoyed writing ad copy and the creative process of working with words, I found writing to be difficult and laborious. Through dogged determination I persevered and continued to write. The descriptive writing for the line drawings of the book is representative of earlier writing; edited for this book.

Within the pages of this book is the story, "Francis, The Uncle I Never Knew." I began with perhaps a few hundred words penned simply as jottings of details and events of my mother's recollection of the death of her brother nearly seventy years before. I knew that if I did not write the details down I would soon forget, like I had done so many times before. Though I had heard the story in bits and pieces a number of times, I am grateful to my mother for her final retelling of the story.

As I thought about Francis, the uncle I never knew, I began to think of what life on the farm must have been like in
the very early part of the 1930's. And so began what became
for me a labor of love.

Writing would never be the same again. Like art, I have
found writing to be another way of expressing my fears and
joys, questions and longings. I began to write quite regularly
and freely; poems and prose of the simple ordinary thoughts
and events of daily living.

"May the wind be ever at your back," is a line from an
Irish blessing. Somehow life, like the wind, is not always that
way. Sometimes having sailed into the wind most of a day I
understand the beauty of the thought however and the need
for rest.

Sailing is for me, a metaphor on life. Sailing into the
wind, known as tacking, working or beating to windward is
exhilarating, fun and some of the most enjoyable work I've
ever done; it's like "you know you are really alive."

And so I invite you on a journey through life and love on
a ship tacking back and forth as we sail our ships among the
stars. Explore the space that is within the pages of this book:
poems, prose and works of art. They are quite simply, reflections, penned in moments of time.

A Distance Traveled

About Galaxy Headings (Chapter Headings)

For readers not familiar with sailing and terms referring to points of sail the following information may be of help.

*The symbol above is found on **even numbered Galaxy headings**. Imagine the solar wind blowing directly down from the top of the page, filling the sails, close hauled, from the left side or port side of the ship. The ship is on a **port tack**; moving forward to the right or starboard.*

*The symbol below is found on **odd numbered Galaxy headings**. The heading of this ship is on a **starboard tack** as the solar wind is filling the sails from the right side or starboard side of the ship. The ship is moving forward to the left or port.*

And so the journey takes us in one direction through the wind into another. And if all this makes no sense to you, know that unless you are sailing it really doesn't matter. I invite you now to relax in your special place and time. Leaf through the pages of this book; read as you wish and enjoy.

A DISTANCE TRAVELED

IN THE LIGHT OF DISTANT SUNS

POEMS, PROSE

& OTHER TREASURES

BY ROBERT BUCKNER

A Distance Traveled

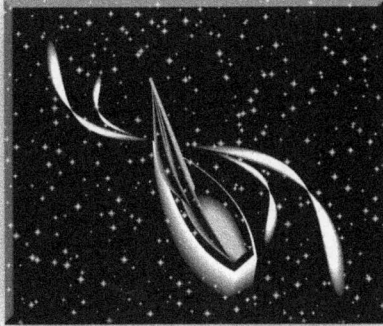

Galaxy 1   For The Love Of Sailing

I came to know and love sailing in the strangest of places. It all began in a cafeteria of a manufacturing plant on the east side of St. Paul, Minnesota. My dad, employed at Whirlpool Corporation, worked as a laborer. Preference was given to sons and daughters of employees and I was hired for temporary work at Whirlpool during the summer before starting college. Work on the assembly lines was monotonous and often times physically demanding. If nothing else the work gave me the incentive to continue my schooling in the hope of a better future.

Working the afternoon shift I often took my dinner break at the plant's cafeteria. On one of the cafeteria walls was a mural. It was a nautical scene of open water, a harbor, blue skies and billowing clouds. Varieties of sailboats, sails set, moving in and out of the harbor; a snapshot of a scene active yet peaceful and relaxing. I usually sat facing the mural. It was for me a wonderful backdrop for daydreaming as I ate my evening meal.

One evening a couple of workers sat down at a table near where I was sitting. In a low, gravel voice one of the men began to tell a story. It was the story of the scene before us. He spoke of the clouds, the winds, the boats and buoys.

I listened as the scene came to life through the knowledge of this man.

Several days later as I carried my tray of food looking for a place to sit I noticed the man with the gravel voice sitting alone at one of the tables nearby. For a kid just out of high school he was a formidable figure of a man with greying crew-cut hair. Having summoned up my courage I asked if he'd mind if I sat down with him at the table. He motioned to the chair next to him and I sat down. I began; "the other day I overheard some of your comments on the sailboats in the mural on the wall." Having broken the ice he began to speak. I listened as again the scene before us came to life. I asked questions and he was ready with the answers. At some point in our conversation we introduced ourselves. His name was Mr. Anderson and in further conversation I realized he lived just down the street from where I lived. His car, a '55 or '56 Buick was sometimes parked near the front of our house.

I visited over dinner with Mr. Anderson a number of times during the eight weeks or so of my summer employment. Through those conversations I learned about yawls, ketches, rigs and sails, buoys and harbors, winds, waves and water.

For Mr. Anderson, sailing was at its best on points of a tack or a reach, in heavy winds with rail in the water. On one occasion he and the crew set sail in some heavy weather on Lake Superior. The boats he sailed were generally fixed keel ocean going yachts. With the boat heeled to the rail and enjoying the speed they noticed a Coast Guard craft approaching. It turned out, because of the heavy weather; they were checking to make sure things were alright.

Much of our conversations were nautical in nature and I learned a great deal about a subject I knew little about. In one of our visits he suggested that I ought to see if I could get a summer job on a Great Lakes freighter. "Wouldn't be any tougher than the work here." He said, "You work and sleep, the pay is good and with meals and a place to sleep included in the deal, a guy can save a good sum of money in just a few months' time." As a younger man he worked the ore ships on the Great Lakes and had sailed the waters of Lake Superior many times. I thought about what he had said from time to time but couldn't quite see myself working a freighter.

I began studies at The School of Associated Art at 344 Summit Avenue in Saint Paul, Minnesota in the fall of '68. (The name has since been changed to the College of Visual Arts or CVA— **www.cva.edu**) With an interest in design I often perused the book stacks of libraries and bookstores looking for books on sailboats, naval architecture and design. I checked out books by Howard I. Chapelle, Nathaniel G. Herreshoff and others. I read with interest the story of Tinkerbelle, a 13.5 foot sailboat and Robert Manry who sailed her across the Atlantic in 1965. Sail Magazine began publication in 1970 and I subscribed to the magazine sometime that year. Later I would come to know of Sir Ernest Shackleton, Tristan Jones, Gerry Spiess, Marlin Bree, Ron Reil and others who's love of sailing and adventure inspired me.

In the early spring of my first year of college I designed and built my first boat in the basement of our family home. It was a modified pram flat bottom boat with a fixed keel built of exterior 1/4" plywood over a simple pine frame. I measured carefully to make sure the boat could be carried up the basement stairs when it came time to haul the finished boat outside.

That summer I learned to sail. I sailed often and my father transported the boat in the family station wagon many times to and from Lake Phalen, about two miles from our house. I sailed as often as I could, usually on a Saturday or Sunday.

September and early October became my favorite times to sail as the winds of autumn grew stronger forming whitecaps on the waves. The sailing was fast and exciting. Now I understood Mr. Anderson's love of the stronger winds.

A Distance Traveled

I remember one late October day heading to the lake with dad. He helped me unload the boat. Stepping the mast and securing the stays I readied the boat for sail. Donning my life jacket I shoved off heading east from the western shore. The 30 mph plus winds blowing from the southwest created whitecap waves as big as any I had seen on the lake. On a broad reach I quickly realized how strong the winds really were. I spilled wind liberally from the sails to keep from capsizing into water that was cold, by now not much more than 50 degrees or so. Nearing the eastern shore I came about, through the wind and headed back again. The plan was for dad to pick me up in four hours time. Rather than returning home my father remained on the shore, watching and waiting. I was grateful. I got out of the boat dragging it from the water.

I walked up to my dad and said, "That's enough." His reply was simply "I thought of telling you it was too windy but you needed to do what you needed to do. " Whenever I asked for my dad's advice he usually gave it as he saw it and most of the time he closed with "...but you need to do what you need to do."

It had been a quick, short sail. Dad helped load the boat into the wagon and we made the short trip home. I was thankful to be back home and thankful I had not capsized into the cold water on that windy October day.

Galaxy 2 — *For This Is Life*

I'm not sure when one really gets good at something. I remember reading the books on how to sail. Sailing seemed rather straightforward, rather simple really, or so I thought. When I finally got my first boat in the water I shoved off into the summer breeze expecting I would simply sail away. Very quickly however, I found my boat grounded, back on shore again. 'Hmm,' I thought, 'this wasn't suppose to happen like this.' I never realized all the nuances of wind, water and a sailboat. Through trial and error, with numerous tries, I was at last free of the shore. I spent the next hours in a steady but light breeze trying to figure out how this sailing thing worked. It was a beginning. For the most part I figured out how to sail. It was only through trial and error though that I was able to finally get it right.

And so I continue to figure it out, this life that I live, much the same as I have always done, through the trials and errors of everyday living. I welcome the fair weather days, and curse the testy, stormy days that come my way, while knowing that I have no choice but to accept with grace, everyday for what it is, life.

BEYOND

Life — beyond our dreaming, our knowledge,
lost in the creases of space and time.
Beyond the atoms,
the strings of illusion and limits of the mind.

Leaves how they scatter
with the touch of the breeze,
carried aloft, thoughts, how they tease,
the newness of life, the places of birth,
simple gifts given, ours to receive,
from unknowing to knowing;
and simply, back again,
into energy and balance,
from a long time ago,
scattered through space,
a future, yet ours to know.

The heat of the day,
to night's coolness gives way,
candles flicker,
filling darkness with light,
and the word of their births,
still now how they linger.
A million light years ago,
stars in the deepness,
now envious of light.

Ah, the wonder, the gift of it all,
into life and conversation,
we all now are drawn,
energy and balance,
from a long time ago,
scattered through space,
a future, ours yet to know.

And cries of new birth
in the darkness are heard,
beyond the atoms,
the strings of illusion and limits of a mind.

Life — simply, beyond.

-rb May, 2011

Thoughts on the poem: Beyond

Once a year parishioners gather in the spring to rake the leaves scattered about, refresh the landscape and remove fallen branches and debris from the grounds of the cemetery. As I worked I meditated on those gone before us, relatives, friends, people of a community of believers who welcomed me into their midst. It was an afternoon of much conversation, meditation along with a few blisters.

I carried the experience of that breezy spring day in my heart and then gentle thoughts of an April day carried into May and emptied onto the page, ink on paper, flowed into the "Beyond."

My mother, as a young girl, on many occasions assisted her dad as he dug the graves in which the departed would be laid to rest. I wonder of the thoughts of my mother, and of her dad, as they worked in the cemetery of the mission church that was their church home.

HOW COULD IT BE

There is a place,
rare and precious,
beautiful beyond imagining,
beyond our dreams or choosing.

This is a place,
where fears dissolve,
like the mist of morning;
where smiles burst forth,
in moments pure and sublime.

This place,
how could it be,
for beauty unfolds,
in visions of deformity.

This is a place of simplicity,
of childlike faith and trust,
where hearts await the rhythm,
of goodness and love.

This is a place of joy,
beyond understanding,
a purity of purpose,
a common ground,
where peace is planted,
and Jesus is found,
in joy and struggle and pain;
simply, profoundly and truly,

in the body and blood of His little ones,
the developmentally disabled and all of us,
the broken.

Bathed, clothed and nourished in LOVE,
we have taken one another's hand
and been led into the HEART of Heaven.

Oh what abounding Love!

-rb April, 2011

*Reflections on the Mpls.- St. Paul Archdiocese Retreat Program
for the Developmentally Disabled.*

Thoughts on the poem: How Could It Be

*Through the years I have opened my heart to those who are handicapped
in some way or another only to discover my own handicaps in life. What
a gift I have been given through the lives and love of the developmentally
and/or physically handicapped persons I have come to know and to love.*

*How often because of my head, my heart has suffered. I have come
to believe that our thinking is a multifaceted process. As such there is a
danger of losing oneself in thought, and left unchecked becomes a prison
from which it is nearly impossible to escape, but for the grace of God's
love. How often I hold the child within me a prisoner of my intellect. I
have found that the retreats for people with "special needs" have been
for me some of the most meaningful times of my life. It is then that I am
allowed to be free of the chains that bind me, the chains of my fear, my
intellect and my doubts.*

*Barb, a sister of my friend Jeff Proulx, was visiting with me about
some of the experiences she had with her younger brother Jeff. Jeff was
born with Down syndrome. She remembered sharing with him some of
the worries and doubts that troubled her. Jeff's reply to her was "Barbie,
just believe." How direct, how pure, how simple in faith, hope and love is
the reply "just believe."*

Her experience with her brother, I believe, is key to understanding the gospel passage: But Jesus said, "Let the children come to me. Don't stop them! For the Kingdom of Heaven belongs to those who are like these children." Matthew 14:19

Father William O'Neil, a priest of the Order of the Most Precious Blood, who I have had the privilege of knowing and working with on so many retreats for the handicapped, taught me a lot. This was a man truly in love with the "Jesus" in the special people he loved so dearly. After having suffered and while still recovering from a debilitating stroke, Father Bill gave a homily at the Archbishop's Mass For Handicapped Persons that I will always remember. In a halting voice and speech audibly affected by the stroke he began the homily with words that went something very close to the following: "I stand here today with you for I am now truly one with you." It is difficult to describe the love radiating within and beyond that sacred time and place.

The retreats continue. Though Father Bill died some years ago, he is not forgotten. I am blessed by the friendship of many who year after year attend the retreats. Some who have worked a year or two, others who have worked for so many. For the attendees, for all of us, as we spend time with the Jesus in the Eucharist, with the love poured out through friends, staff and volunteers, it is a precious time indeed.

I think of the brevity of this life and the promise of the eternal life. To all who have been a part of the retreats, to their families and loved ones, I dedicate the poem, "How Could This Be."

INTRODUCTION

Bare Branches *The Essence Of Life*

The story Bare Branches is edited and adapted from the text of the original essay.

"A Case For God" was the theme of an essay contest sponsored by America Magazine – published by the Jesuits. The contest was open to writers of all ages and occupations. The essay was written in April–May of 2008. The time spent with the writing of this essay was for me an opportunity to grow as a writer and most importantly to grow in my faith.

It is Love, the "bare branches" of our lives from which the buds of life unfold.

This photo was taken on a frosty winter's morning on my parent's farm.

A Distance Traveled
Bare Branches
The Essence Of Life

What if I, like Helen Keller, were unable to observe the stars against the black of a night sky, or the rising and setting of the sun? Would the stars still not exist, the sun still rise and set?

My friend Ken died on a Friday, the last day of September 1983. He was working construction and in the noisy environment of the site a dump truck backed over him. I was devastated as I received the news. It was two and a half years previous, almost to the day that my father died. Memories welled within and replayed as I grieved the loss of my friend.

I thought back to a family visit with Lottie and Ken on their farm when I was a young man still in high school. It was in the early evening. Lottie left the barn to visit with mom while Ken continued with the milking and chores. I scraped the walks and did what chores I could. I listened as Ken and my father continued in conversation. They visited about struggles with drinking and Alcoholics Anonymous; a relatively new and developing program at the time. I remember their discussion about the various aspects of the program so helpful to so many who suffer from addiction. I remember in particular the discussion referencing spirituality and prayer.

As I listened, what struck me at the time was how well they seemed to know and understand one another. My father, like Ken, worked as a farmer, logger and construction worker in the years before he married. In many ways they both shared similar life experiences. They both suffered their own life struggles and it was a common bond that gave strength to their friendship.

And so it was at the funeral service for my father, as I walked from the church I noticed Ken, sitting in a pew, sobbing uncontrollably. How he must have loved him.

A few months later Ken and Lottie stopped by to visit with my mother. I was digging into sodden earth, unplugging drain tiles at the farm home where my mother continued to live. Ken joined me on the project and both of us, on our knees, worked side-by-side clearing the mud and replacing broken tiles. As we worked, mud up to our elbows, we visited. As we shared our stories the pain and loss at the death of my father was lessened.

And now, with the news of the death of Ken, the pain and longing returned, the embers of grief again flamed to life. Seeking solace and consolation I attended an evening prayer service on Sunday, October 2nd. That evening in memory of St. Francis our prayer gathering came to a close with the Peace Prayer. Caught up in grief at the death of Ken, in my inner pain and desolation all I could think was; 'I don't know that I believe anymore.'

A search for God

For me, for most all of us, questions abound. What do I believe? How? Why? Is it really important to know the answers? Will I ever find the answer and if I do, what will I do, how will I feel? I remember quite clearly sitting on the front steps of my home as a young boy wondering how it was I came into existence. Where did I come from? How does a life come into awareness? As I wrote, I wondered about some of my earliest of thoughts, are these indeed the memories of that earlier time? Often, as a father I am intrigued and surprised to hear the comments and questions of my own children. Why shouldn't the questions of one's youth accompany us as we journey through life? Why should the depth of thought come as such a surprise? And so my life has been in part a journey in search of answers.

The Bible, written down through the ages, more than two thousand years translated from languages no longer spoken, of people, of cultures we understand only through the portal of anthropological study and history. Many people simply point to the Bible and say "There it is, the answer to the questions found on the printed page. See it, speak it, and hear it, the inspired Word of God, the Holy Bible." How I do wish sometimes that it was that simple, but for me it is not that way.

Today, I read a newspaper or magazine and know from experience that what is written and printed is not necessarily true. As people of faith the Bible holds within it the truths of our faith. For me, "Proof of God" through the simple reading of the printed word disintegrates without the prejudice of a faith journey. Mere words are of little value if they are not lived out in our lives. If we speak the word we must live the word. Without participation, words are only words without the power to transform us.

I remember one evening reading the first words in the Gospel of John "Light from light, true God from true God, begotten not made" also a part of the Nicene Creed. I reflected on the word and the thought of God as light; the eternal light. The theory of relativity came to mind. Einstein, through intellect and an imaginative mind, theorized that at the speed of light time no longer exists. "The eternal God," I thought. How intriguing, how ironic that scientific theory in reference to light in a sense supports the "Light Eternal" referenced in the Gospel of John.

We often fear science will prove God irrelevant or worse yet, non-existent. I believe God is irrelevant to science only because of the nature of God, as Spirit, as Love; God cannot be tested through scientific measurements, calculations or observations. In relevance to John's gospel "Light from light…" perhaps Einstein came as close as anyone to hinting of God's existence.

Science questions and searches for truth. Religion, viewed by some not to be questioned, is a search for truth. What is the truth? Science cannot change the truth nor can religious thought change the truth. The scientist, if in fact he or she believes in a God, does not bring God into their work, for God is without measure. And yet as time goes on, science is finding exponentially more questions than answers. It is as if scientists also find themselves working with the eternal, the immeasurable.

All experience as a human being is in a sense a living language. We see, read, measure and experience each other, our world, universe, all creation and ourselves. Like words our lives are in flux and change through time. Old Testament passages speak of stars in the heavens. There is a connection with ancient peoples as we look at the night sky and observe the light of those same stars. Through the progression of time and knowledge the vocabulary of stars has been made known to us. First the telescope made images from starlight clearer. Eventually, astronomy developed other ways to sense or listen to the language of stars, and the known vocabulary of the entire universe is ever increasing.

During the last century so much of what was only thought to exist has just recently been observed and verified. What was only once imagined between the pages of a science fiction book is now a part of our everyday existence.

If God cannot be seen, heard or measured through scientific means, what then? As I thought deeper about a purely nonphysical world, Helen Keller came to mind. A college psychology professor at the art school I attended once asked our class, "If you had a choice to see or hear; which would you choose?" Not surprisingly in a class of artists the overwhelming response was to see. Then the professor went on to talk about the strong connection of hearing and emotions. He then asked the same question and I realized on that day, a choice between the two would be far more difficult than I had imagined. Blind and deaf, what Helen Keller did with her remaining senses is incredible. Helen Keller felt her heart beating within her, blood coursing through her veins, the air filling her lungs, the aroma of life that surrounded her. Helen with the love and patience of her tutor, Annie Sullivan, was able to see without seeing, to hear without hearing. I close my eyes and feel a piece of pottery and in a sense I can see. Sound through vibration I also feel but the connection does not seem nearly as direct.

What if I, like Helen Keller, were unable to observe the stars against the black of a night sky, or the rising and setting of the sun? Would not the stars still exist, the sun still rise and set? For Helen Keller the sun never rose or set in a visual sense. Helen Keller's illness at the age of nineteen months resulted in the loss of her sight and hearing. Though she did not see the sun, she felt its warmth and in the cool of the night perhaps imagined the twinkling of starlight. She would know of stars only through the eyes of others. The sounds of night time and of the daytime were shrouded in silence. Helen Keller's life speaks to me of the possibility to see beyond our human nature into the unknown. And so we, like her, do the best we can with what we're given. We all live with our handicaps as well as our blessings. Helen Keller faced a choice, either live in the chaos of her disabilities or have faith in the abilities with which she was blessed. Helen Keller in 1941 is quoted "Life is either a daring adventure or nothing." Within that simple line I see and hear her faith.

I was blessed by the life and love of Mary Kraemer, a Franciscan Sister of Little Falls, Minnesota, who as a young woman due to illness, lost her hearing and lived much of the rest of her life in a wheelchair. However there are few people I know with more zest for life than she. Mary embraced faith, hope and love and the promise of the Word of God. She was funny, imaginative, loved to write and was independent with an infectious spirit. The gift of her smile still lifts my spirit. She worked for years with the deaf community in the diocese where she lived. Her lip reading was so proficient most times I forgot that she was deaf. When she was diagnosed with terminal cancer, confined to the care of others she asked to see me. We visited one more time. Later that night I awoke from my slumber. It was through my sadness and longing that love entered in. And so on that moonlit winter's night I penned the prayer poem "Smile Upon Me."*(Page 55)*

The poem, in a very real sense is Mary's gift to me the writer and you the reader, a gift of love that is of God. Faith, hope and love are the gifts we are given and ours to pass on.

In the most difficult of times God's love and care enters my heart. I began this essay with the remembrance of the death of Ken. It was at his funeral, as I stood at the grave site, full of doubt and despair, that God again touched my life in very ordinary ways. A flight of geese heading south to a winter's home and the presence of another beside me were God's gift to me on that day. *(A detailed account is found on page 47 within the story – "Treasured Moments")*

As I traveled home later that day, reflecting on all that had happened at the burial service of Ken I suddenly came to the realization that it was October 4th, the Feast Day of St. Francis of Assisi. Yes, all that had happened was indeed a blessing in the most unexpected of ways. It was for me an "Emmaus Moment." And to think that only a couple of days before I had gathered in prayer with friends, struggling in silence with the question, 'I don't know that I believe anymore.'

We all have within us incredible moments when we experience life in some special way. Whether or not we see the works of God in our lives is quite another matter. I believe that in time we will come to know God, the love that is the essence and the gift of our lives.

All that I experience speaks to me of life in fullness and carries forward into unending creation.

...Unending Creation

The love I receive
is the love that I share
is the beauty I seek
the poverty I feel
the stillness that calls
the heart that aches
the child in my arms
the stranger I meet
The song I sing
the vision I paint
the words that I write
in celebration and love of life
come from the God within
and the God without
the God who caresses
and cradles in love
the soul not afraid
that dares to seek
and to know love
the experience of a moment
or a lifetime
how blessed to know love
to know God
who works in us
and through us
Always.

And so I am content to live in the mystery of the moment with faith, hope and love. We are a people present, past and still to become, a part of the unending creation, in the light of distant suns.

"Things which eye has not seen and ear has not heard, and which have not entered the heart of man, all that God has prepared for those who love him." **1 Corinthians 2:9**

Through reason alone to say that God exists or to say there is no God is I believe quite impossible. In the last analysis we must travel beyond thought into the mystery of love. For whether we do or do not believe, we are called by Jesus to love one another. And a life lived in Love simply is of I AM WHO I AM.

"So faith, hope, love remain, these three; but the greatest of these is love." **1 Corinthians 13:13**

It is Love, its barest branches and the essence of whom we are, from which the buds of life unfold.

I wish to acknowledge and am grateful to good friends who read the original manuscript offering suggestions, edits and encouragement as I wrote the essay. Thank you to David, Thomas, Dick and Rosemarie for gifts of time and talent.

-Sarah B. 2012

STARS IN THE DEEP

Blossoms of sweet clover,
a sprinkling of starlight,
and the patterns now I see,
as stars in the deep of a galaxy.
How wondrous the vision,
that opens our eyes,
to another's point of view.
-rb

Thoughts on the poem: Stars In The Deep

It was a showing at a coffee house in Menominee, Wisconsin that I first viewed the picture above. The black & white photo, simple and lovely was taken by my niece Sarah. How like the stars I thought and stars are what they became as part of the cover of this book. The poem, "Stars In The Deep" was inspired by the photo and to Sarah I dedicate the poem. Thank you Sarah! And to the staff and all who volunteer and provide support at The Arc of Dunn County, Wisconsin – for your advocacy, vision and work; Thank you!   ***http://www.arcofdunncounty.org***

OUR CALVARY

Dance in the darkness, oh candle of light,
whisperer of softness, transforming the night.
The heavens reflected in waters below,
in mystery, in darkness, new life aglow.

Through silence and darkness, travel, I must.
Weakened and weary, stumbling I fall,
no longer able to carry it all.

Bathed by my tears, dried by the touch
of whispering wind and love's gentle hush,
the music of nature, the calling of leaves.

Through silence and darkness, travel I must.
Weakened and weary, stumbling I fall,
no longer able to carry it all.
Where is my helper, my lover and friend?
In arms that embrace me, I am lifted again,
above mists of misery, the absence of love.

Through silence and darkness, travel I must.
Weakened and weary, stumbling I fall,
no longer able to carry it all.
The stranger, the beggar, the enemy I fear.
The lost, the forsaken, the words that I hear.
Whose arms will embrace me, now, in this fall?

In darkness and silence I lie where I fall.
Where is the whisper, the candle of light?
Oh Love, oh my longing,
in silence please hear,
the voice of my calling on the deafness of ears.

Oh Love, oh my longing,
in the darkness please see,
a body that's broken, in pain and misery.

Oh Lord, this life, our Calvary.

In darkness and silence there is no reprieve.
The veil is now lifted, in the light of the day,
my sisters, my brothers, clearly I see,
you who I feared, are so very much like me.

-rb Thoughts at a northwoods cabin, September, 2010

Thoughts on the poem: Our Calvary

I had recently received material in the mail that I felt to be hurtful to good people who I know and have known who are gay or lesbian. The package containing the video lay on the end table in the living room of our home; unopened. It contained a DVD I had already viewed at my church and online as well. Try as I might I could not find much good to say about the presentation but that perhaps it might serve as a beginning for dialogue about who we are as people, as church.

I was feeling rather out of sorts by it all, saddened not only by the mailing itself but that it was sent by leaders of my church. Often, when I am feeling out of sorts I take some time away from the everyday routine. Usually what is bothering me resolves as I relax and enjoy some time away from the daily grind. As it happened, the annual fall fishing trip to the cabin of a friend of mine was on the calendar. A good buddy and I began the road trip to a little red cabin on a northern Minnesota lake. We would meet up with the rest of the possums (our fishing buddies) who were already there.

Quintessentially Americana, the cabin was built in the fifties at the edge of woodlands overlooking the lake. In our forays of the big woods of the area we have seen the signs of big cats, deer, bear and all sorts of creatures inhabiting the forestlands of northern Minnesota. The cries of loons and the scream of the eagle can be heard by day, the hoot of the owl by night

Arriving at the cabin on a glorious fall afternoon we were soon out on the lake where tensions release but for the line on a pole. I enjoy fishing but mostly I enjoy the immersion into nature, the sounds and sights and the beauty that surrounds.

As the sun slid behind the western hills, the lake now like a mirror, the pallet of the setting sun's colors reflected in the waters below. The dusk continued and the blue of the sky deepened. The brighter celestial bodies and stars kissed the surface of still waters. The sky and the earth became as one.

With the boat secured to the dock we followed the sloping path to the dim glow of light from the cabin. Fish were filleted, supper prepared, a fine meal was enjoyed. Card play, a few drinks, some reading and conversation completed the evening activities and soon it was off to the bunks and beds for a good night's rest. Some days I fish, some days I hike or mix it up. And so goes the ritual of days at the cabin in the fall.

Morning came and it was cloudy, a bit misty as I recall, a nice enough day to do some fishing or writing as the spirit moved. On this day I would choose the latter. Relaxed in a comfortable chair, coffee cup in hand I thought back to the previous evening on the lake. The first stanza of the poem "Our Calvary" came easy.

> *Dance in the darkness, oh candle of light,*
> *whisperer of softness, transforming the night.*
> *The heavens reflected in waters below,*
> *in mystery, in darkness, new life aglow.*

Several hours later having finished my writing, I recited the poem to the guys with the understanding that it was still a work in progress. There were a few words of comment after the reading and in silence I packed the legal pad and pen into my bag. I would do some edits and make a few changes later back at home.

As I penned and scratched and penned some more, the thought occurred to me that just as Jesus trod the rough way to Calvary, we too, as church and as individuals must do the same in our own time. Jesus did all that he could for those that he loved. He did not deserve the sentence he suffered, death on a cross. The suffering endured by Jesus was for love alone. Love one another, in humble service, wash one another's feet, these were some of the last words from His lips in the last days before He died.

So what was it that was heavy on my mind as I wrote the poem and tried to make sense of it all? 'Why,' I asked, 'is someone different from myself, not accepted for who they are, rather than who I or someone else thinks' they should be?' If a person is not acting so as to hurt anyone, but to love someone, how is what they do somehow wrong? As a society, government, church, are we justified in hiding behind our customs, rules or laws at the expense of another?

And so it is in love that I live and follow in the footsteps of my Lord as best I can. Jesus knew our humanity and His acceptance of the cross was the ultimate act of forgiveness, mercy and love for all. I, in my own little ways, must live my life of forgiveness, mercy and love as I know Jesus to be in my own place and time. In joy I follow my heart where it leads me, without fear or anger, knowing and trusting in the Love of God and sharing that love with my sister, my brother.

Galaxy 3   *In The Company Of Friends*

I built my third sailboat in the machine shed on a farm located near Lake Elmo, Minnesota during the spring and summer of 1980. Sixteen feet in length, a day-sailor with a Cuddy cabin, the boat was built of marine grade plywood over clear fir framing. For nearly seven months I worked on the boat whenever I could. Albert and Caroline, retired from dairy farming, were usually about and I would often visit for a while before going to work. They would lend a helping hand whenever assistance was needed as the work progressed. Friends on occasion accompanied me or stopped by and their assistance was always appreciated. I rigged and finished the boat nearing the end of May 1981.

When my cousin Carol learned to walk she would exclaim in delight "Whee"as she stepped her way across the floor. My dad nicknamed Carol "Little Whee." Traditionally boats are referenced in the feminine form and carry feminine names. It is the notion that the sea will mother and protect the boat on its journey just as a mother protects her child.

And so it was, on a beautiful June day in 1981, friends and family gathered at Lake Gervais in St. Paul, Minnesota for a picnic and the christening of the new sailboat. And in honor of my father who had passed away three months earlier and in keeping with the tradition of the naming of a boat my mother poured a few sips of champagne on the boat's bow and christened it, "Little Whee."

I had promised Albert a sailboat ride sometime after the boat was finished. And so a year later Albert and I set out with the boat in tow for the city of Hudson and the St. Croix River to do some sailing. It was an overcast, breezy day as we crossed the river bridge. I could see occasional whitecaps below. "It might get a bit rough today," I said. "Are you sure you want to go sailing?" Albert, well into his seventies, assured me he was good to go.

With the boat in the water, rigged and ready, I gave Albert a quick course in tending the jib lines before setting sail. We headed south into the wind. Albert seemed a natural as he tended the lines of the jib sail. What a day of sailing it was. We were soon under the bridge and sailing in one of the widest areas of the St. Croix River. We tacked, through the wind coming about many times as we continued our sail down river. Little Whee had never sailed better. There was an easy, rhythmic motion as the bow lifted and then dropped, the wood vibrating in a mellow tone cutting through the waves and spray often caught by the wind was sent our way. It was pure delight.

My concerns for Albert's comfort vanished as we continued our sail. I sensed Albert rather enjoyed the exhilaration of the sail. I was amazed at his agility and the ease with which he moved one side of the boat to another as tack after tack we made our way. After perhaps a couple of hours of beating to windward we came about, setting the sails for a mix of runs and broad reaches, we sailed our way back to the city docks.

I have spent many days and a handful of nights sailing in the company of family and friends. Each sail is unique not only for the variability of the winds and waters but the uniqueness of who we are as people. I invite you now to continue the journey "In The Company Of Friends."

How Like A Dream

How like a dream you are
from so distant a time now.
Your sweetness of voice,
eyes that searched and knew me,
and a smile that lingers into forever.
You sit beside me,
giving comfort even as I write.

Elizabeth; this little girl I knew.
Betsy, you loved to hear that name,
for it was you and it was yours,
as if there was no other.

You listened to the stories we read,
of a God who loved us.
You knew so much more than I
For love was yours, the treasure you shared,
The gift you so freely gave.

Never did it seem,
anything wrong in Betsy's world.
and yet so very much was.
Your sweet face, disfigured,
and a heart that would beat
but for a short while longer in this world,
unless by some miracle…

One in ten were the odds
that you would make it through
the surgeries to come.

I know now that it was
"Through Him, with Him and in Him"
that I came to know the Jesus in you Betsy,
and in all those who knew and loved you.
Their lives must have been changed,
for my life is forever changed because of you.
That is how we are for one another.

Jesus on the night of His birth was
"wrapped in swaddling clothes"
by His Mother, Mary.
Jesus now wraps us all,
wondrously, in Mercy and in Love,
in this world and the next.

-rb   April, 2011

Thoughts on the poem: How Like A Dream

The seeds of thought within this poem lie dormant within me for many years and go back to the time of my youth. St. Patrick's Parish on the east side of Saint Paul, Minnesota, was the faith community that gave welcome to our family. As a teenager I was a member of a program for youth; the Junior Legion of Mary. Fr. Paul Dudley (who later served the church as a bishop) was the associate pastor of our parish and our youth director.

As a group we met regularly for prayer and meetings, enjoying many fun times together. Through our work we came to know and love many people within our parish family. As young people we took on assignments given by Father. Usually, in teams of two, we were assigned to visit the homes of the elderly, shut-ins and families who were caring for a child or adult with an illness. Joe, my team partner had been a good friend since early grade school.

One of our assignments was to visit a foster home in our neighborhood. Elizabeth was one of six or seven young people with developmental and/or physical disabilities who lived in the foster home. As I recall, Elizabeth and one of the other children in the home were Catholic, though often several other children gathered with us as we welcomed all. Joe and I visited the children regularly as catechists during the school year. They were always happy to see us and we were truly happy to see them. We took turns reading or sometimes read together the biblical stories; commentaries and questions within the religious education text books provided to us and enjoyed many wonderful discussions. To this day I remember Elisabeth's voice, soft and gentle as she read the Gospel stories. My heart was touched by Elizabeth and all who lived with her in a special home filled with hope and love.

Years later, I was invited to work as a volunteer at a retreat for developmentally disabled adults in the Archdiocese of Saint Paul/Minneapolis and have continued to work on the retreats every year since, but for one. During these retreats I am often reminded of the incredible gift of love God gives to us all.

I think back to the foster home where I first encountered God in the childlike faith and trust of persons with disabilities. Through the years I have remembered often those who I have met, worked with, cared for and have come to know and love. I continue on with joy in my heart, trusting in the goodness and love of God. St. Paul writes.... "Nothing can separate us from the Love of God in Christ." Romans 8:38-39

How beautiful, how comforting is the Word of God.

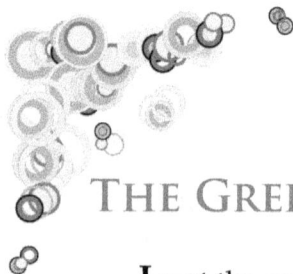

THE GREETER

I met the greeter today,
there, to bless, and to be blessed.

I met the greeter today,
in the beauty that surrounds me,
in family and friends and people I know.

I met the greeter today,
in the music, measures both difficult and easy,
to sing, to play, to dance, to love, to embrace.

I met the greeter today,
hands and fingers dancing on keys,
listen to the embrace, the greeting.

I met the greeter today in another I know,
and the ones I have yet to know,
the caregivers at a bedside,
medicine and gowns.

And there, in a sterile room, to greet me,
humor and pain surround.

Goodness and care sustain you, and you, me.
I wonder, at our meeting, you and I,
greeters to one another.

Vessels of love we are, poured out, empty,
knowing love's smile will greet us again.

Through stubborn birth
into dusty days you greeted me.
and sheltered me in a mother's loving arms,
a father's care.

Tired, I rested awhile and walked again,
the paths you have shown me,
the paths I have come to know,
the paths I have yet to know.

The brown cover now draped,
the book of music closed,
longing for another time,
another moment's pause.
The memories and the music of love
now resonate from within,
a vessel of clay now ready for the pouring,
for the greeter.

Take leave my joy and rest until another time.
For there will be another time.

I met the greeter today,
there, to bless, and to be blessed.

-rb   Reflections on the day, June 26, 2010

Thoughts on the poem: The Greeter

I joined with the choir of St. Thomas Aquinas for warm ups prior to the 10:30 Sunday morning mass. There are times when I struggle with the notes, timing, lyrics or one of many nuances to be found in the music we sing. The beauty of a choir is that voices blend and minor imperfections are made perfect by the multitude of voices that surround. And so, I gathered with my friends on this Sunday morning of June 26th, 2010, to sing and to celebrate the Eucharist.

Later that afternoon I traveled to Regions Hospital in St. Paul to visit a brother-in-law, Greg Smith.

The greeter at the information desk that afternoon was truly a messenger (an angel) of love. I asked for Greg's room number. In but a moment the information I needed was accessed and wrote down on a visitor's note pad. Removing the note from the pad he gave it to me. I stood for a moment looking at the information, quizzically I'm sure. He stood up, came around from the desk and through voice and motion showed me the way to the elevators that would take me to the floor of Greg's room. I thanked him and went on my way.

Just down from the information desk in the open hall, overlooking the lower lobby area, a woman sat, playing the piano. I stopped to listen, she finished, closed her music book and looking up smiled at me. "That was very lovely," I said. "Thank you," she replied. We visited for a few moments. I then continued on my way.

Greg, seriously ill, greeted me as I entered his room, happy to see me. We visited in voice, in silence and in presence. Hospital personnel came and left during my stay. All who entered the room brought love, comfort and care to Greg as well as myself. I remained with him for perhaps an hour or two, and then we each said our goodbye and I left the room.

As I was leaving, I noticed the piano, keys now covered, silent, and the music book closed. I continued on my way and noticed too, the information desk, the empty chairs, the greeter gone, the day's work of love, done.

Later that evening I wrote the poem "The Greeter" as I reflected on the experiences of a beautiful summer day in June.

What a difference one person, one life, one greeter can make in the life of another.

I dedicate the poem "The Greeter" to the volunteers, staff and medical personnel of Regions Hospital in St. Paul, Minnesota and in loving memory of Greg Smith, my sister Ramona's dear friend and husband who died in September of 2011.

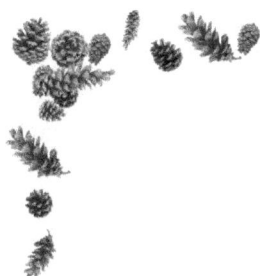

JEFF PROULX

"Lord Jesus, on a wonderful weekend such as this I am beginning to know just a little bit of your wondrous love – so many wonderful and beautiful signs in the handicapped who are my friends. Lord, we are all handicapped and your love fulfills our dreams and diminishes the handicaps of our lives.

Thank You, for all these, my friends: To Jeff, John, Ed, Agnus, Dorothy, Grandma, Carol, John, Maggie, Terri, Ernie, the Dear Sisters and Father Regi. Thank you for Joy, Love and Peace, here in this place."

(The lines above are from an entry I made into my journal while on a Journal Retreat for persons with developmental handicaps – November 12, 1983)

September 14, 2009

I came to know Jeff through Ernie Forss and Journal Retreats for persons with special needs which were developed by Ernie, while working on his Master of Arts in Religious Education at the University of St. Thomas.

Jeff Proulx is in my thoughts these days, thoughts that fill my heart with joy for he was and is a sign of God's wondrous love.

Jeff always strived in life to be normal, to be one of the guys. He never would, nor could he be normal, for he was extraordinary. Jeff's was a life full to the brim with love poured out by family, neighbors and friends. Jeff would carry that love with him through his life and quite literally spill love to all those he would meet, across a nation and a world. Jeff was truly a vessel of God's Love.

Jeff poured love on my life, my family and friends and in time, those who I would come to know and love. Jeff served at our wedding mass on the day Barb and I married. When our third and last child Andrew was born, Jeff was the Godfather we chose, along with my sister Geraldine, the Godmother, as our newborn son was welcomed into the Christian family through baptism.

The life of Jeffrey, memories that continue in my thoughts; simple, profound, incredible moments of life, of love and of forgiveness, selflessness, understanding, compassion, volumes of virtues and a life fully shared. Like etchings on finest crystal glass, now broken, the Fire of God's Eternal Love will melt and create anew, Eternal Life for Jeff. Such is the Love of Our God.

With family gathered around, Fr. Jerry anointed with Holy Oil, our brother Jeff, who lay in his hospital bed so sick and so weary. His mother, Helen, and family gathered around to bring comfort and love. The Living Gospel of Jesus was alive in our hearts, in that room on that day.

I thought of our brother, Saint Francis of Assisi who made the Gospel of Love truly real in his life and the lives of us all. Jeff's faith, like that of Francis, was simply a faith lived in the life of LOVE, of JESUS!

Listed in the obituary under the name Jeffrey Raymond Proulx is written, "Angels danced the day you were born."

Born with Down syndrome, Jeff's life transcended all the difficulties and struggles he faced. He grew in wisdom and grace and gave us all the courage to live beyond the limits and handicaps of our own lives. He taught us to believe in ourselves, the gifts we have, to trust and know the power of Love.

Indeed, angels danced the day he was born for they knew the great love of his mother, Helen and the family of his birth. Angels danced the day he died for he is with them now and all whom he loved and who have gone before him and there are no difficulties and struggles, for he shares fully in the wondrous Love of God.

No, Jeffrey Raymond Proulx could never have been normal, for he was extraordinary. As God is with us, so too is Jeff in our hearts, all the days of our lives.

Who was Jeff? The following are but a few Jeff snippets... snippets of forgiveness...like the day I called and said I would pick Jeff up at his downtown St. Paul apartment one evening. We would be going out for dinner and a walk. Well, I forgot and did not remember until the following day. I called, apologized and he said, "It's alright Bob, I forgive you."

And the time we drove to the cabin and cleaned under the crawl space beneath the cabin floor. We then washed up in Cohen Creek, and went for a hike, enjoying the pine barrens of Wisconsin. The both of us ended up with a rather serious case of skin rashes caused by poison ivy. Jeff's mother took him to the doctor twice for treatment. I felt so bad about the whole ordeal. I knew it was bad, for I had rashes and blistering on about a third of my body. Neither Jeff nor Helen ever complained to me; though weeks later we shared our stories.

Jeff played ball with the family and enjoyed backyard bon-fires, roasting hotdogs and making S'mores. I enjoy to this day the replays of a video Barb took of the bunch of us playing football one afternoon.

If I spoke disrespectful of anyone, and there were times I did, Jeff would call me on it and would only say "Bob!" With little more than a few words of acknowledgement peace and harmony were quickly restored.

Jeff was my helper on so many occasions, at the shop, our home, and at the Minnesota State Fair, assisting, always helping in any way he could.

Jeff enjoyed the Minnesota State Fair and it became an annual tradition for us. It was a day to walk, eat and see it all. We visited the barns, and worked the Moo Booth on several occasions. The Fine Arts building, the 4H building and the political stands were all part of the mix. Politicians; Jeff had his favorites and exercised his right to vote. As a proud employee at 3M; the 3M exhibit in the Progress Center – *Eco*

Experience at the fair, for a number of years, was a must stop and introductions were made to whoever was staffing the exhibit at the time. And finally near the end of the day we'd relax and enjoy a beer, talk about our day at the fair and anything else that came to mind.

Jeff was very much like a brother to me. When I asked Jeff what he thought about this or that, if his reply was, "not much" it was clear and I knew the subject was of little interest to Jeff. End of discussion. I always knew our conversation was on track when I heard the emphatic "Oh Yes!" A good time would be guaranteed without a doubt. The "Oh Yes's" were life for Jeff.

Church and Jeff's prayer life were most important to him. And for Jeff the totality of his life was prayer. He was a member of Mary Queen of Peace Fraternity in covenant with The Franciscan Brothers of Peace and was a professed member of the Secular Franciscan Order. The Mary Queen of Peace Fraternity was founded by Daniel Berry, a dear friend to both Jeff and I, our families and to so many whose lives were blessed by the goodness and talents of this remarkable man.

A lifelong member of Saint Patrick's Church in St. Paul, Minnesota, Jeff was active as an altar server and usher. He was a model of welcoming to all people, without prejudice.

Scouting and The Order of the Arrow, outdoor activities, high adventure and world travel were most especially on Jeff's "Oh Yes" list.

"Oh Yes," was Jeff's cheer for life. I can hear it now, 'O-H-Y-E-S, Yeeeaaah Life!' He was a cheerleader for so many programs and activities, always out there participating with all his heart, never one to sit on the sidelines.

Jeff enjoyed and was an active participant in so many sports: including bowling, floor hockey, swimming and golf. He especially enjoyed the Special Olympics. Jeff had a wall full of ribbons, medals and awards, recognizing his accomplishments and sportsmanship in the many and varied sports activities in which he participated.

Jeff enjoyed art and often worked at his drawing board, gifting his works of art to family and friends. Jeff enjoyed playing music on his keyboard which was an important part of his room or apartment furnishings. His oldest brother Richard Proulx, a well-known organist and composer of liturgical music, was especially close to Jeff in heart and spirit.

Jeff, the youngest child of six was nurtured in love and Jeff mirrored love throughout his life of 52 years. Jeff reached out to others and others reached out to Jeff. I have known no one with a more natural intelligence for social etiquette than Jeff. I was humbled many times by his ways with people, his respect and his quick assessments of the need of another. Visits with friends, relatives and celebrations of special occasions filled his social calendar.

Because of the unselfish love of so many caring people and a loving family, Jeff was able to travel the world and to enjoy independent living for a good many years. Throughout the thirty plus years that I knew Jeff, he spoke to me often of the respect and love he had for all of his brothers and sisters, his mother, father, nieces, nephews and friends.

Jeff's family lived in the same neighborhood as my family, attended St. Patrick's Church and its school on St. Paul's east side. I knew of the Proulx family since I was a young man and remember a few brief visits with Jeff's brother Jim in those days. I was not, however, aware of Jim's brother Jeff at the time.

In 1983 I said "Yes," assisting Ernie Forss on a Journal Retreat for developmentally handicapped persons. If not for that "yes" and the work of Ernie perhaps I would never have met Jeff, our dear friend who taught us so very much.

Jeff's was an extraordinary life of love, lived in simple ways and lived to the very fullest.

This story of Jeff was penned on September 14, 2009 – the anniversary of our wedding. Barb, I and the boys consider Jeff as one of our family. Jeff served at our Nuptial Mass and is Godfather to our third son Andrew who was the inspiration for the poem featured on the next page of this book, "Monkey On My Back."

MONKEY ON MY BACK

Monkey on my back,
hang on, don't let go.
You are my friend,
not just a another
monkey I know.

Let's swing in the trees,
enjoying the breeze,
of a summer afternoon.

So make a friend
and get to know,
the monkey on your back.

-rb

LOVE'S MOMENT

There's a comfort in the night,
in darkness deep
with wondrous resolution.

One by one, stars that gave light,
direction and comfort to the night,
suddenly transformed into the light
of a new and brilliant day.

In sacred darkness,
light eternal mixed with time,
your life and mine.

And now, suddenly, you are gone.
In my longing, tears stream down.

Love's moment,
voice soft, touch tender,
light eternal mixes with time,
once again, your life and mine.

There's a comfort in the night,
countless stars that guide me,
God's promise, of loving arms that carry me
into the light of new and brilliant days.

In Love's arms, I now know rest.

-rb March 19, 2012

A Distance Traveled

Thoughts on the poem: Love's Moment

John Berschens was a farmer, as was his father and his grand-father before him. The farm located on the south side of Lake Jane in Lake Elmo, Minnesota had been in the family for four genera-tions. John's way was direct, honest, a man of the earth. In the thirty years that I knew John I visited with him no more than a dozen times. John was related to Caroline, wife of Albert Eberhard on whose farm I built my boat, Little Whee.

I read the Pioneer Press Paper the morning following his death on March 17, 2011. As John was crossing Highway 36 north of Lake Elmo and west of Stillwater he was struck in the dark of the evening by a car driven by a young woman. It was a tragedy for the Berschens family and that of the young woman and her family as well. I was truly saddened by the news. Only days before, John had come to mind and I had decided to visit John on his farm in the spring.

I wrote the poem "Love's Moment" a day or two following John's death. It is the promise of and the light of everlasting love that transcends the ordinary in our lives.

It was a snowy morning on the Wednesday of March 23rd, as I set off to attend the Mass of Christian Burial at St. Mary's Church in Stillwater, Minnesota. As I traveled the snowy roads I wondered how many people would brave the weather and the drive to Stillwater for the Funeral Mass. I stepped into the church and it was full, with people seated and standing in the back vestibule.

As the prayers of the faithful were read for John, nearing the end of the prayers the reader indicated that at the request of Jan, John's wife, the following prayer be read. (I paraphrase) 'We pray for the driver of the car that struck John, and for her family. May God give them peace and healing; we pray to the Lord.' What a beautiful prayer from one heart to another heart.

Here was a man, a family man, a 74 year old farmer who lived his life in simple ways and a church filled with people who came together to honor the life of this remarkable and good man. Some-day it will be spring and we will meet again John Berschens.

Galaxy 4 *Ordinary Days, Loving Ways*

I was visiting my dad one evening at Veteran's Hospital in Minneapolis, Minnesota a few days before his death on March 29, 1981. It was an ordinary visit, much of it in silence but there are a couple of lines I remember as if it were yesterday. I had completed the building of my third sailboat Little Whee only the fall before. "Son," he began, "you're not thinking of sailing your boat across the ocean, are you?" Taken aback, I fumbled for a reply, looking for an escape clause. "No, not that one Dad," I said. His reply, "Good." The thought however had crossed my mind a time or two and he knew it.

Weeks later I was visiting with my mom on the farm. At some point she told me how one warm sunny day in October my father spent an afternoon on board the boat, examining it from bow to stern. It was a lovely day and he sat for a long while before climbing out and heading back to the house.

I don't know that he said anything to mom about the boat, but that he spent time in review of the boat for so long was good enough for me. I learned in a passive way the art and skill of woodworking from Dad as I watched him at work in his shop as a boy, sometimes for hours at a time. Time spent with one another; so ordinary, so precious.

WILDERNESS SNOWMAN

Time spent building snow people are to be treasured for it is time spent with those we love. And I remember one winter, dad taught us kids the game of Fox and Geese. In un-trodden snow he walked in a shuffling manner creating a circle perhaps forty or so feet in diameter. Then he divided the circle into half, quarters and eighths in like manner. The place in the middle of the circle where the paths met was the place of safety for the Geese. A Fox was chosen and so the Fox chased the Geese in a game of tag.

One day, many years later, I would play the same game while on a date with a young lady. And less than two years later we married. Some years later I asked my wife, Barb, what it was that gave her the idea that she would marry me. "The first time we played Fox and Geese at the cabin" was her reply. It was a wonderful weekend with family and friends. And so a word of caution about the game; it could change your life.

Thanks Dad!

TREASURED MOMENTS

My youngest boys, Brian and Andrew had been begging me to go to the cabin. It had been some years since they had been there. It is a cabin on five acres of woods in the pine barrens of Wisconsin. The cabin had fallen into disrepair after years of neglect. Recently I have begun to repair the cabin so that we could again enjoy some time with family and friends, especially in the wintertime of the year.

One a Saturday, the early part of April, we headed to the cabin – there remained a few inches of snow in the woods surrounding the cabin. We hiked on trails for several miles. We followed along the ridge of what I call the Trade River Gorge. We began where Cohen Creek empties into the Trade River, that empties into the St. Croix River some three or four miles further. There were no complaints from the boys as we hiked and that is in itself a minor miracle.

Brian had found a walking stick at one point and we continued further on – exploring springs gurgling from the earth and looking for the tracks left by critters in the snow. We saw several deer and found wild turkey tracks. We then began to make our way back and as we walked Brian turned to me and inquired, "Jesus, he was kind of like a superhero wasn't he dad?" What a wonderful sharing, a rare treasured moment. It was one of those moments you long to share with a child but seldom does it happen in such a spontaneous, free and uninhibited kind of way. Andrew had gone ahead and so Brian and I conversed together for some time.

A week or two later, in the early evening, Brian, Andrew and I were at home in the living room. I don't recall watching TV at the time and I don't believe the boys were playing video games as they often do. Brian was relaxing on the couch, Andrew was sitting on the carpet busy with something, and kids it seems are most always busy with something. Brian asked, "When people pray does God talk to them?" I was startled by his question.

After an awkward moment or so and a bit of fumbling for the words to say, I then began sharing with them a story about the death of a dear friend, who I came to know for he was a good friend of my father. Though much younger than my Dad, Ken died in a construction accident not long after the death of my Dad. I recalled how after Dad's death I grew very close to Ken. One day after Dad's funeral Ken and his cousin Lottie stopped to see my mom on the farm. Lottie was a friend of my mom's. Mom and Lottie had remained good friends since the time of World War II when they worked on the railroad yards in Superior, Wisconsin and met as young women in their early twenties.

It was on a weekend and I had traveled to the farm to see my mom. I was outside dealing with a laundry tub drain field. The tile had become clogged with mud that had seeped through broken drain tiles and the laundry tubs would not empty. Ken came to my assistance and we dug and worked in the muck side by side. We had the most wonderful talk as we worked removing and replacing tiles, mud up to our elbows. I thought to myself, 'Ok God, my Dad is gone but now Ken is here beside me. Thank You God for Ken.'

One day the phone rang. I was told that Ken had died. When I heard the news I at first refused to believe it was true. Then I became angry and then sad. Ken died on Friday, the last day of September 1982. On Sunday evening October 2nd I went to a prayer gathering at Brady Retreat Center (TEC). Since the Feast of St. Francis was on Tuesday, October 4th, the evening ended with the prayer of St. Francis, "...and it is in dying that we are born into eternal life." I sat in silence, empty as though God had let me down. I was still angry with God for allowing Ken to die so suddenly and tragically in the accident. I thought, 'God, I don't even know if I believe anymore.'

On Tuesday morning I traveled to Cornell, WI to attend the funeral. A minister had graciously offered his services for the family and officiated at a prayer service in the funeral home. It was a very nice service, complete with a wonderful homily. With much sadness in my heart, we followed the hearse to a cemetery along the banks of the Chippewa River.

There was a large gathering of mourners present. The minister stooped, took the dirt from the newly dug grave in his hand and simply said, "Dust we are and into dust we return," while sprinkling the casket with the dirt. Nothing more was said and there was silence. As I stood there I began to hear the honking of geese far in the distance. Looking to the north I saw three formations making their way south, flying toward where we stood. As the geese continued, they began moving out of the three formations and in their passing over the cemetery had formed one very large V formation. It was as if we all were awakened into life again and people began talking to one another. I turned to the person on my right; suddenly I realized who he was. "Are you Gus I asked?" "Are you Bob?" he replied. I had not even noticed he was standing by my side.

Gus was an architect from Chicago, Illinois and every fall for many years had come to hunt with Ken. Ken had said to me many times, "Someday I'll have to introduce you to Gus, I think you would have a lot to share." That day Gus and I became friends.

(After attending the funeral of Ken I wrote down the basic details of October 4th, 1982, so as to never forget the remarkable experiences of that day; the Feast Day of Saint Francis of Assisi. I have read the account a number of times since.)

"Brian," I said, "People sometimes do hear a voice. For me however, God answered my prayers in other very special ways." I added, "And then on the way home I suddenly realized that it was the Feast Day of Francis of Assisi who's prayer I had recited just a couple of days before with so much doubt in my heart."

I was finished with the answer to Brian's question. Both boys had amazingly sat and listened to what was a lengthy answer to Brian's question, "When people pray does God talk to them?"

Andrew spoke first, "So God speaks to us through people." "Yes, that's right" I replied. 'Wow,' I thought, 'he's got it.'

Then Brian said, "Dad, I had an experience when God answered a prayer. It was my first time as a server at Mass. After Communion I sat thinking about the mistakes I had made while serving. I asked God to give me a sign that I did OK. Do you know near the end of Mass Father announced that this was my first time as an altar server and didn't I do a great job serving for the first time. And then the people applauded. God answered my prayer."

I did not share the following with the boys on the evening of our conversation about prayer and how God answers them, but would like to share with you, my friend, as the following I feel is particularly meaningful and is an important part of my friend Ken's life

As a young man I would travel to Cornell as often as I could and shared many wonderful times with Ken and Lottie. Lottie's husband John died in the mid-fifties leaving Lottie with three kids and the farm. Lottie continued to farm. Ken, a cousin of Lottie's offered to help her on the farm soon after the death of her husband. Ken was an alcoholic at the time and as I understand had severe problems with alcohol addiction. Lottie was a very direct lady who always spoke her mind; one of the reasons she was so endearing. "Ken, I would welcome your help but if I catch you with even one drink, pack your bags and you're gone." Ken worked with Lottie for many years after the death of her husband John. He never to my knowledge had another drink. He helped with the work and also helped Lottie raise her two daughters and a son.

The times we spent as families and friends were many and blessed. I treasure the gift of his life and the times we shared. Truly God blessed me with Ken and Lottie and so many others.

And you, my friend and minister in the Lord, we as a church are blessed by you as pastor. Thanks so much for the courage of sharing your faith, for your homilies, and for your love and care for God's people. Thank you so much for answering the call to minister. I do think of you often. I thank God that you are a part of my life. We all struggle in life, I know, for all of us have had our own share of struggles and yet continue forward with hope. You were very much in our prayers as a family last year as you went through the months of help and healing that you sought for alcohol addiction. We prayed for you often.

Continued love, prayers and peace!   Bob B.

LOVE'S EMBRACE

What a precious gift
the life we are given
the paths we take
creation, our lover
holding us tight.

Look to the heavens
in wonder and celebration
of a love so deep
so all consuming.

How can it be?

Held tight
in love's embrace
beauty surrounds
entering deep within
the whole
of who we are.

-rb

Thoughts on the poem: Love's Embrace

I have come to know and believe in love. Love is always embracing, for love has no choice but to embrace. Love is simply all that we are and all that we know. I believe without love, we simply would not exist.

How much of my life has been spent chasing love, as if it were something that I had yet to receive or to know. It's like the dog that chases its tail, I was just unaware. And so I laugh at the dog and forgive myself. As I have lived, love has been my constant companion, all along.

In the early spring of 1980 my cousin Gloris and her husband Norris, invited mom and dad to Nebraska to visit relatives. Gloris and Norris were so pleased when they accepted the invitation. While my dad's family moved from Nebraska to Wisconsin when he was just a boy, most of his cousins and relatives remained in Nebraska.

And so Barb, George (Ray), Gloris and Norris took off in Norris' Cessna 172 Cardinal. My dad as a young man in the 1930s often flew with his good friend Joe, in a small two seater single engine plane. I can only imagine how my father must have enjoyed flying again. My mother I'm sure found some comfort with Gloris by her side. From all accounts the trip was quite an adventure, with wind, bumpy air, rain and all. They were happy to see and visit with quite a few of dad's cousins and friends.

I love the picture of the two of them, Dad with his quizzical smile and Mom, just a bit shy. Gloris and Norris gave so many gifts of love to our family through the years. This photo and the trip to Nebraska was another gift given, another gift of Love's Embrace.

Dad and Mom
On a flying adventure with Gloris and Norris visiting family in Nebraska

LIFE IN THE BALANCE

Wind driven rains
mother bird on her nest
wind ruffled feathers
chicks warmed by her breast.

Mercy she calls
and weeps in her pain
mixes and falls
tears with the rain.

Life in the balance
as the fierce winds blow
memory's quick glances
of some time ago.

Warmth that still lingers
long after that storm
of a mother that kept her
so safe and so warm.

And now in her time
to feel and to share
the warmth and the love
of a mother who cared.

When the storm is over
how can they know
'til one day again
the fierce winds blow.

-rb

Thoughts on the poem: Life In The Balance

The poem was written reflecting on the life of my mother, her mother, my grandma, indeed all mothers and women. Life is a most precious gift and the costs and sacrifices made for the lives of the children are truly of God.

This line drawing was originally commissioned for a greeting card honoring mothers and all women who share without measure the beauty and wonder of this life and the life beyond.

STORIES

Somehow familiar
the stories I hear,
like thunder's echo
rolling across the land.
Echoes that travel farther still,
even across the days, the years,
generations past and still to come.

Stories; gateways to hearts
yearning for love and belonging,
How simple, yet so intrinsically woven
within the complexities of our being.

Stories of tenderness and love,
of fear and of pain,
of losses, of failure and gain.

Like rain upon dry parched earth,
stories have quenched our thirst.

-rb *Reflections on the day, July 17, 2011*

Thoughts on the poem: Stories

Sometimes out of nowhere the writing begins and "Stories" is one such poem. This poem was penned in the heart of the summertime, at a time when the land thirsts, sporadic summer rains fall and the lightning changes the nitrogen of the air into fertilizer for plants; the thunder rolls. Thoughts and a summer rainstorm struck a chord.

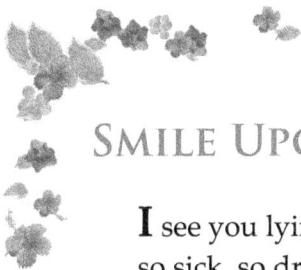

SMILE UPON ME

I see you lying there,
so sick, so drowsy, so weary.
I must talk to God I say.
But what do I say?

For some prayer,
is why I awake, in the
deep of the night.
But what do I say?
I think of you lying there.
I wonder –
Is God with you?
Unseen in the dimness
and shadows of your night.

I look out the window.
Bare branches.
Moon, its reflected light.
Sun soft.
Patterns of light,
painted on the cold canvas
of snow below.
And it is beautiful!
This life!

This life!
But a moonlit night.
A promise
of the light of day,
which is to come.
Ours – because we Are.

God visits us in our darkness,
in our nights,
as God does
And as God did last night.

Miss you?
I will, when you are gone,
having answered life's call.

And when I talk you will hear,
as you always have,
and smile upon me as
You always do.

-rb   January 2003

In memory of Sr. Mary Kraemer
Born, April 3, 1937 - Died, February 13, 2003

Thoughts on the poem: Smile Upon Me

I first met Sr. Mary Kraemer at a retreat for the hearing impaired. I was invited to work at the retreat serving meals, cleaning, and spending time in prayer with other volunteers. It was Mary's smile that first captivated me. She lit up the room and I watched as person after person came up to her. She brought a smile to all she met.

A motorized wheelchair was her way of getting around. Her lip reading was remarkable and the truth is most of the time when visiting with her I forgot she was deaf. Through illness as a young woman Mary lost her hearing and the movement of her legs. She was the founder of religious education for the hearing impaired of the Archdiocese of St. Paul/ Minneapolis and authored many religious textbooks. She ministered as a director of Teens Encounter Christ (TEC) retreats and programs for the deaf and was a director of Come Aside and Rest Awhile.

Not long after I got word that Sr. Mary had died I met with a client for lunch. We knew each other well and I felt comfortable in sharing with him the poem. He read the poem. "Nice" he said. I wasn't expecting what he would say next. "Did you share this poem with Sr. Mary?" I had not thought to share the poem with her. I had, however, hoped to see her again before she died but I never did.

Sr. Mary was a woman with many gifts and she was an exceptional writer. As I entered the poem into this book, I recalled a little book Sr. Mary had written and so I did an on-line search. I found the book listed within the web site of her Franciscan order. Sr. Mary's religious order, the Franciscan Sisters of Little Falls, is in Little Falls, Minnesota.

*Sr. Mary's book is delightful. If you wish to purchase her book visit the sister's web site **http://www.fslf.org** - within the site - (subject to change) point to **"Contact Us"** and on the drop down menu click **Franciscan Gift Shop** - click on **books** and you will find Sr. Mary's book **"Inwords"** or call **320-632-0601***

"Inwords" by Sr. Mary Kraemer - A playful volume dealing with words within words as a prayer form based on Ecclesiastes 3:1-8.

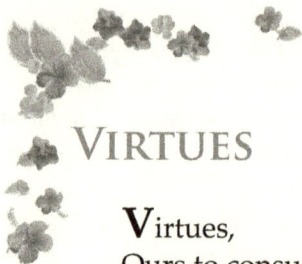

VIRTUES

Virtues,
Ours to consume,
To make us whole.
Energy that sustains,
The mind, body and will,
The beating of hearts,
The rhythm of lives.
Lies, like thistles grow.
Honesty — chokes the thistle, sooths our pain.

Alienation, the fog rolls in.
Unity — we were together all along.

Hurt, as an ember burns.
Forgiveness — the ointment of healing.

Failure, seeds planted, longing for life.
Perseverance — the rain that sprouts forth seeds
of **Success**.

Broken, lives longing to belong.
Integrity — the glue that forms and holds us
tight.

Adversity, trees bend, breaking in the winds.
Assertiveness — stand tall with strength,
in **Knowledge**.

Virtues — words, painted on a wall,
To be seen,
To bathe,

To feed,
To clothe.

Indifference, chasms that separate.
Understanding — the bridge built in
Caring for another.

Arrogance, power, fear one another.
Humility — knows the gift of self,
in **Service** to another.

Closed, as petals in the night.
Truthfulness — in the light of our days,
the fragrance of who we are releases.

Life is our gift to give.
Responsibility — ours to learn, to know, to **LIVE**.

Fifty eight thousand, one hundred and ninety five.
The number of names engraved on a wall,
Shouting, pleading, praying, crying, **Peace**,
Compassion, **Courage**, **Love**, weeping, wiping
tears from cold black granite stone. In another
place and time, still we remain **Hopeful**, wait with
Patience, And **Trust** that **Justice** and **Goodness**
prevail for all people one day.
And war and violence shall be no more.

Virtues, words painted, on a wall.

-rb November 2009

*The poem Virtues, is dedicated to all who work at Community of Peace
Academy Charter School, St. Paul, MN. To all who study and play within
its walls – past, present, future, I wish a life of peace and fulfillment.*

*In memory of, and with gratitude for the life of Pfc. Kham See Xiong,
class of 2004. Long after we're gone, Love, the essence of who we are, remains.*

Thoughts on the poem: Virtues – and a vision.

In the late summer of 2009 I took on the assignment of painting virtues in words on the walls of the new and recently completed high school addition of Community of Peace Academy (CPA). The words are painted on wall space above the lockers located on each of four floors. Other graphics are painted in a variety of interior spaces and the vision statement of CPA is painted on the walls of the main high school entrance stairwell, from the top floor to the main level entrance doors.

One day as I was standing on a ladder happily painting the letters of one of some forty virtues, the assistant principal of the high school, Rob, asked me, "how is it going?" I acknowledged that I was doing well and that as I painted the words of a virtue I thought about each of their meaning and what they meant to me in my life. Rob's reply was something like "That could be interesting." Teachers came and went in the week before the start of the school year. They usually had words of affirmation and encouragement for me as they passed by. I continued on in the hope of finishing the "Virtues" project before the opening day of the school year.

A month or two after completing the work of painting the words and the graphics on the walls of the school I took some time and penned the poem "Virtues." It was at about this time when a CPA alum, Kham See Xiong, of St. Paul, MN, was shot and killed during the tragedy at the Fort Hood military base in Texas, one of twelve soldiers who died by a horrific act of violence on that day. I thought back to the many young soldiers of my generation who lost their lives in the Vietnam war. The Vietnam Memorial Wall and so many more memorials amplify the terrible cost of war in lives lost and the importance of virtue in our lives and of living in peace with one another.

On the east side of St. Paul, Minnesota, St. Patrick's Church and its Catholic grade school served to educate young people and their families. The school was staffed primarily by the Sisters of St. Joseph Carondelet. I attended classes from the third grade to the eighth grade at St. Patrick's. Some fifteen years later the school closed and the parish struggled for another fifteen years to find a suitable use for the building.

During this time a young woman working in the field of education had a vision for a charter school. Her vision for this new school... "At Community of Peace Academy, our desired outcome is to educate *the whole person — mind, body and will — for peace, justice, freedom, compassion, wholeness and fullness of life for all." In 1995 Dr. Karen Rusthoven established CPA in what was once St. Patrick's grade school.*

Since then a variety of specialized classrooms, libraries, and a gymnasium, with one of the first "green roofs" (a roof partially or completely covered with vegetation and a growing medium) in the state of Minnesota, have been added to the original grade school building. The school continues to serve the youth of the neighborhood and surrounding communities, offering a quality educational experience for the students. CPA works with families as well as its students to help ensure their future success. It is peace that gives hope to our families, communities, nation and world.

In the early spring of 2010 I was given the honor of designing a CPA Memorial on the east facing wall of the school's "Green Roof" Memorial Garden, honoring Kham See Xiong and in time future alumni and friends of CPA. His wife, family members, alumni, staff and friends of CPA were present at the May 2010 dedication of the Memorial Garden wall.

My special thanks to Mike Pearson and the staff for their expertise and assistance with the memorial project. Mike and I first met as students at the College Of Visual Art.

A CHRISTMAS GIFT

"**B**obby, time to wake up!" I kept hearing the gentle but firming voice in the fog of sleep. "Time to get up, time to get up." The voice, as if in a dream, kept repeating over and over and I began to feel the gentle nudge of a hand on my shoulder as at last I roused from my slumber. "Sorry to awaken you from your sleep" Mom said, "but you asked that I wake you when it was time to get ready for the Midnight Mass."

Now that I have children of my own I marvel at the patience and persistence of my mother. That she was able to wake me from my sleep at that time of the night, as most parents know, could be called a "Christmas Miracle."

The walk to church, about half a mile or so, was cold and the stars were bright in the dark of a midnight sky. We entered the doors to the church of St. Thomas Aquinas and made our way down the steps and into the warm glow of the basement sanctuary. We took our place in the pews amid friends and neighbors.

Evergreens surrounded the stable in which the figurine of the baby Jesus would soon be laid. The stable was dark. One by one the candles were lit and the Christmas Midnight Mass began. To me it was simply a night secure in the love of a parent, beautiful music, light and a stable filled with the wondering of a child.

The figurine of the baby Jesus was placed in the manger and the single light in the stable was now aglow. The Mass ended and I hurried to the stable. The sight and smells, the earthy ambience of bark, sticks and straw, linger on in memory to this day.

As we walked home, I wondered about the present that would greet me in the morning to come. I was sure that a toy electric train, like the ones I'd seen in the windows of a store would be waiting for me. I climbed the stairs and entered the simple half walled upper room. I crawled into bed and was soon asleep.

I awoke in the very early morning, my sisters and brothers still asleep. I made my way down the darkened stairway. The kitchen light was on and the tree lights were glowing. There on a table by the front window sat a caboose, a boxcar, a tanker and flatcar, a coal tender and engine on a simple oval track. And then I saw it, the key to a wind-up train.

I can still remember as I gazed with disappointment at the gift I was given on that Christmas morning. My dad came over from the kitchen and flipped the lever on the toy engine and the train began to move. I watched it as it made the rounds. After a few times around the track and with the energy in the spring spent, the train with its simple metal cars on the simple oval track came to a halt. Much like the spring so too was my spirit spent. My dad lifted the engine, took the key, wound the spring and placed the engine on the track. "Now you push the lever," he said. I gave the lever a push and the engine derailed. The wheels spun and the train just sat there. Dad quickly shut the engine off and again placed it on the track. He pushed the lever and after a round or so again the train came to a stop. Giving me the key he said, "Now you try it." I could not hide my disappointment any longer. "I can't turn it!" I said, "It's too hard! I hate wind-up trains." Never one to give up, dad again took the engine, wound the spring and placed it on the track. Dad continued to work patiently with an ungrateful boy and eventually I worked through my disappointment of that Christmas morning.

I think now about how he must have felt on that Christmas morning. He was not always so patient a dad and looking back, his patience that Christmas was a gift.

Our family moved later that year to St. Paul, Minnesota closer to dad's work. Dad worked as a laborer at a factory job for the last twenty years of his working life. When he retired dad and mom put their home up for sale in St. Paul. They moved into the quite primitive farm house in rural western Wisconsin. It was the home of my mom's parents, a place of freedom and love, where we spent some of our summers. For me it was a place of happy memories.

For a while I lived at our parents' home in the city with some of my brothers and sisters until the home was sold. I then rented an apartment and having recently graduated from art school was working at a job as an artist. Those earlier years working as an artist were lean and challenging with months of layoffs and working odd jobs. It was during those years that I began to understand how difficult it must have been for my parents.

My parents barely made ends meet. Dad worked in a factory and I can still hear him groaning, suffering from back pain caused by a herniated disk in his lower spine. I remember my mother and I, seven or eight at the time, trying to pull dad up and out of bed. Most times he steeled himself and managed to go to work. Some months later he under-went what at the time was very risky back surgery. In those days layoffs and strikes were almost cyclical and made life for them even tougher. With help from friends and family in times of greatest need, and government food surplus pro-grams mom and dad kept the family going. As more kids arrived, eight of us in all, a laborer's paycheck was not quite enough. Mom took on jobs when there was no other choice and with her skill at managing the household finances, and her working from time to time, there was somehow always enough. I marvel at their persistence, resourcefulness, their faith and love, the glue that held the family together.

Years later, I would recall the Christmas morning and the gift of a wind-up train. I was moved to tears as I thought of the preciousness of the gift and the sacrifice my parents made to buy that simple wind-up train. Some twenty years later love had found me in the memories of that Christmas past.

And love continues to visit, not only at Christmas time, but every day, if I but open my arms and heart to receive the gift of family, friend and stranger. I remember my parents and the gift of love they were and are for me. I remember all who have been a gift to me as I journey in this life. I pray for all who are in need and that I open my eyes to recognize their need and that I may respond in love, all the days of my life. I pray for you who read this Christmas remembrance that you be gifted with love for it is in love that we are truly blessed.

FLEETING THOUGHTS

Traveling forward,
follow the sunset of the artist's palette.
What beauty surrounds,
never the night.

Traveling backward,
follow the sunrise, always the morning,
never the day.

Imagine, dreamlike,
traveling as the heavens do,
though ever close to this earth.
Never the night,
never the day,
always the sunset
always the sunrise.

Through the blue and the fogs of mist,
one thousand miles and more an hour,
counter to a spinning earth;
exhilarating, no doubt.

I am content
to take my rest
to travel the miles
on a spaceship called Earth,
to experience the day and night,
the heavens above and the earth below.

-rb January 19, 2012

Reflections on the poem: Fleeting Thoughts

What is a youngster to do in Minnesota when the calendar says January and the sport so loved is baseball? Work out in a warm place I suppose and so that is where I found myself on a Monday night in the month of January. I had brought my son Andy, for a winter's evening batting practice to an indoor sports facility. To while away the time, I brought my pad and a pen. I sat down in a lobby area and began write.

Recently the sunsets and sunrises had been particularly beautiful. The sunrises, transforming darkness into light and the sunsets, light into darkness, giving measure to the days and the nights and to our lives. The Earth spins on its axis as the movement of ever changing clouds and the beams of sunlight filter through the atmosphere, spraying the skies with the beauty of color. The dynamics of these ever changing events are measured in mere minutes.

What if the sunsets were measured in hours or days rather than minutes? How fun would that be if only for a time.

It was during my college years as I studied art and design that I was first introduced to Buckminster Fuller. He came to mind as I penned the poem. Through the years I have read and enjoyed several books by "Bucky" Fuller. In one of his books he describes standing, at the time of the sun's setting, feet planted firmly upon the ground, facing north, the sun in the corner of your eye, legs and arms outstretched, parallel with Earth's latitudes. Fuller wrote. "I want you to really feel this with me. Earth, this enormous sphere, revolving on its axis with incredible speed and quiet motion." "Bucky" as he is affectionately nicknamed was an incredibly imaginative guy. He helped to popularize the term "spaceship earth" and engineered the geodesic dome, structures iconic of the Epcot Center, and the Expo 67 Montreal World's Fair. Today geodesic domes and structures are ubiquitous throughout the world. Buckminster Fuller developed and brought to life geodesic type structures, and so many other designs through his imaginative thinking and the playful work of a lifetime.

So, these were some of the warming thoughts on a cool January day that filled my head as I wrote the poem "Fleeting Thoughts" reflecting on a winter sunset.

ONE STAR

One star amidst the billions of stars
one moment of time
amidst the eons of time
light and time converge
eternity is glimpsed.

What is the measure of a life?
Life, a star amidst the billions of stars
the light that glows,
warm red or bright blue
in the twinkling of an eye
or an evening's flickering flame
the sunrise and sunset
of a million years
are but a promise
of another tomorrow.

And so we slumber
awaiting the light
of the one star
amidst the billions
a dwarf among the giants
the star that gives light
and measure to our days.

-rb

Thoughts on the poem: One Star

The seeds of this poem were planted in my thoughts one Sunday morning as I joined with my "choir family." The readings of that Sunday morning inspired the poem "One Star." This poem is penned for all who have lived lives of service, in simple, humble and loving ways.

Galaxy 5   *Ghosting Along*

In sailing terms to "ghost" is to move along in times when there is no perceptible wind. Often the winds of summer get lazy. With sails set and little if any wind to fill them, a boat appears to be still in the water. Looking over the rail towards the bow, ripples on the surface of the water flowing out from the bow indicate a boat is actually moving, though ever so slowly. The boat is said to be ghosting along.

I remember one of those disheartening sailor days. It was on a small lake east of St. Paul with my first boat, an eight foot pram. It was one of those lazy summer days with barely a breeze. I watched as a sailor on a boat nearly twice as long as mine stood on the deck of his boat, at the fore of the mast and with hands grasping the mast, leaned to one side and then the other. The main sail set, close hauled, would fill, empty and fill again and so back and forth across the lake it went. There was a rhythm to the sailor's movement and I watched with interest and admiration of the sailor as the boat moved forward from one side of the lake to the other. The sailor was making the best of it, getting his exercise and having fun too. And so I worked on my sculling skills using the tiller and rudder of my little pram. Sometimes to be in a boat on the water, is its own fun even though one gets nowhere, slowly.

Sometimes, when for whatever reason life isn't going as planned, it's time to do whatever it takes to move forward and create our own opportunities. Early on in my art career I found myself out of work and looking for a job. It was a disappointing time in my life as I searched for work. I decided to do some pen and ink drawings along with some descriptive writing in an effort to lift my sagging spirit and keep moving forward. It was indeed good therapy.

Eventually I found work again and continued on with my career. Later the next year I received an added bonus for my efforts during my time of layoff. I was paid by a printer for the rights to use the line drawings presented on the next twelve pages, as art for a calendar.

And so, life has a way of renewing itself much like a fresh breeze on the waters. I invite you to Galaxy 5 • Ghosting Along. If you have ever experienced living, working or playing among the ghosts of barns and agricultural structures on the farms of years gone by, then relax awhile, and travel back in time.

If you have never had the privilege and pleasure of experiencing life on a farm then consider this your first visit. If you ever get the chance consider a visit to a real farm. In so many important ways the experience remains the same today as yesterday.

Sheltered Contentment

Upon entering a barn no longer used as a shelter for cattle, memories of the heart bring to life the warmth of another place and time.

As autumn changes to winter and the days become shorter, the nights longer, the barn becomes a sanctuary to cattle both day and night. On a cold winter evening a feeling of peace and tranquility permeates all around as the senses take in the surroundings of the barn. The soft jingle of chain, cows in the stanchions, the subtle sound of movement as hay is pulled loose and eaten, the rhythm of breathing, the smell of the hay, the straw, a complexity of odors surround and mix in the warmed air. Bare incandescent bulbs burn bright, creating both light and shadow. The radio crackles with static. The barn, wonderfully warmed by the life which it shelters.

Deep Silence

The snow had come and gone this day and with it the winds which have smoothed the contours of the land into drifts subtle and deceiving.

The night sky now clear, the moon shining down, seemingly bright like the day, reflecting the light of the sun and casting moonlight and shadows on the snow below. The air is cold and harsh yet somehow inviting. As I stand, listening to the silence which I hardly knew was there, the cold is sharp on my face. This is a night with a beauty all its own.

I stand for a moment more, feeling, watching and listening, wondering how the life of summer survives the extremes of winter. As if pushed by some unknown force, I begin my way to the barn, knowing that life and warmth await me inside on such a cold, and long winter's night.

The Hill

High on a hill the windmill stands, the winds of many seasons having brought its blades into motion, turning gear and shaft, pumping water from the earth. The melodic song of motion, driven by wind, has pumped cold fresh water to many a thirsty person and watered countless heads of cattle.

Birds have built their homes on its wood platform, oil soaked from years of use. Its ladder has been climbed many times for the oiling of its mechanism, or by the daring of a youngster.

Its frame structure of steel and bolts have withstood the buffeting of heavy winds, rain, sleet and snow. And often the lightning of a summer's storm has sought its way through steel to ground.

Patiently the windmill waits for the calling of the wind.

The Farm Gate

The old wire farm gate is representative of the strength, work and ingenuity of the farmer. A gate such as this is as strong, effective and economical a gate as can be assembled.

Appearing as if timeless, the wire farm gate would tell many stories if it were able. Stories about those who twisted its wire and set its posts, those who opened and closed it countless numbers of times, the cattle which have passed through it, the seasons which it has endured. The gate stands, the wood of its posts slowly decaying, wire rusting, someday to be replaced or be lost but for the memories.

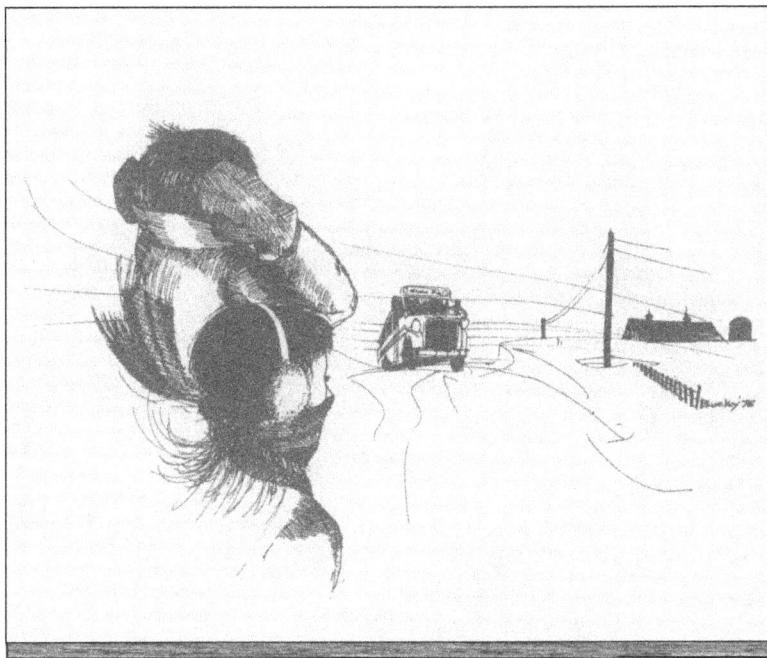

A Welcome Sight

What a welcome sight! The school bus carries within it, warmth and good friends to the students who await its coming on cold and windy winter mornings.

The school buses make their way along the routes, roads sometimes half buried under drifts of windblown snow. Day after day the ritual continues throughout the school year. Bus stop after bus stop, students board, the bus fills and students arrive safely to school. Friendships are formed, and memories cherished as like wheels on a bus, the years roll quickly by.

Weathering Of Time

Traveling through the countryside scattered here and there, can be found buildings and homesteads from out of the past, abandoned and of seemingly no use except as a recording of time.

At one time these buildings and the land surrounding them had been a part of someone's life, good and useful buildings filled with the hopes and dreams, sadness and joy, toil and hardship of lives not much different than yours or mine.

Now, weathered by years of exposure to the elements and in grave need of repair they stand. They tell the story of another place and time if only we understood the language of these buildings left behind. Buildings that whisper, we too are growing old.

The Hay Door

As the summer passes by, the mows fill one by one, wagon load after wagon load, bale after bale, until bales are stacked to the roof.

From inside the mow the view of the countryside, through the open door, would present itself as the hay neared the slanting roof over each mow. Finally the last mow nearest the big door would fill. With the view from the door there came sometimes a breeze but always a little more sweat, for it got hotter as bales piled closer to the roof.

Later, when there was as much hay as could be stuffed into the peaks of the mows the big door would be pulled up by rope through a pulley. The hay would be protected from the rains of autumn and the snows of winter until the following spring, mows nearly empty, the door would open for the hay of another summer's harvest.

Evening Tranquility

There is something comforting and serene as I travel the country roads of my youth. The silhouette of barn roofs against an evening sky and farmhouse lights aglow beckon to me as I pass by. It is a peaceful scene in a sometimes all too stormy and chaotic world. It is a way of life, which like many others, must be experienced to understand.

The rural landscapes I have known have changed greatly through the years. One thing remains, farm families continue to work and care for the land and the life they love while providing food for a nation and world.

Autumn Field

The moon casts its glow over the dark dank soil of what's left of a corn field. The imprints of tires on the soil, the mark of knives on corn stubble, and a few standing stalks of corn are all that remains to tell the story of another autumn harvest.

The soil is soft and easy under my feet. The chilled night air is restless and alive, exhilarating! The leaves rustle in the breeze and sounds amplify all around. On a night like this the dying and decaying autumn is changed. A sense of renewed strength permeates from the surroundings, removing doubt, anxiety and loneliness which present themselves at times. Sometimes I wish these nights of autumn would last forever and in a sense they do, for it is the yearly harvest that feeds us.

Winter will soon be upon us. The memory and harvest of autumn will sustain and see us through until the next harvest moon.

The Hay Chute

As the pastures give up their youth, seed and die, fall gives way to winter and the cattle once more are brought into the barn where they will remain until the coming of spring. The mow filled with the summer's harvest of hay now begins to empty.

On a cold early winter night after milking is done, the hay chute door is slid open. Above, hay is stacked to the roof. Formations of frost hang above and all around as the crude ladder is climbed. It is like climbing into a place of fantasy. The warm air below rises and meets with the cold air above, and the mist freezes and gathers. Stopping for a moment, looking through the cracks in the siding of the mow, the sky is clear and the stars illuminate the night sky.

Bales of hay are pulled loose from their lofty perches and tumble to the floor. Look out below!

Waiting For Morning

After a hot afternoon, the last load of hay would be pulled up to the barn. The unloading of the hay could wait until the morning. There was still more to do until the day's chores were through.

Down to the milk house we would go for a drink of water from the watering hose. More water found its way on us than in us, it felt so good. Then it was up to the house for supper, and down to the barn for the evening milking. The chores now done, it was into the car for the short ride to the lake and a swim before the sun went down. After the swim it was into the car again for the ride home in the cooling night air. How wonderful that would be after the heat of the day!

Finally, into the sack, for tomorrow would be another day just as beautiful as the day which had past. Feeling the night breeze through an open window we drifted off to sleep.

The Monument

The barn which stood, partner to the silo, is gone but for the remains of concrete and stone. The cattle which it sheltered, gone too.

This silo will probably never again hold within its walls the sweet corn silage that was fed to the cattle through the cold days of winter. Nor will the howl of the blower fan which filled it be heard or the scratching of the fork and pick removing frozen silage from cold concrete walls.

Straight and tall as when it was built, the silo shows its age in the weathering wood, rusting hardware, and the scarring and cracking of cement wall.

Through days of sunshine and storms, and the ever changing seasons of the years it still stands, now but a relic of the past, a symbol of another time and the ever changing rural landscape. A monument to a life on the farm that once was.

LIVE LIFE

Live life
To the fullest
Without fear
Of what may come
Knowing that life itself is enough
Love, laugh, enjoy.

And so one day wandering a pasture,
I snapped this photo...
and I loved, laughed and enjoyed.

-rb

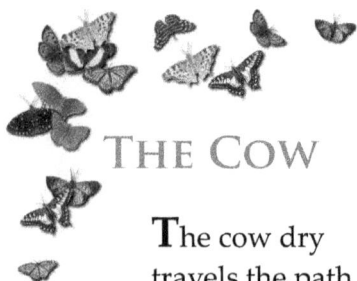

THE COW

The cow dry
travels the path
familiar and worn

In a shelter
from rain
no more
now emptied
comforted only
by the fragrance
of earth

-rb

Galaxy 6   *The Joy Of A Journey*

Joy, I find, is in the experience of the journey and through faith, I believe joy is our destination. I've never sailed a boat on an ocean and the thought of towering waves, relentless winds and the chaos of a storm at sea frightens me. Tristan Jones was a sailor, adventurer and writer I came to know through his writing. I remember the first time I heard him speak. It was on July 7, 1995 in an archived interview with Terry Gross (NPR "Fresh Air") broadcast following his death on June 21, 1995; with great interest I listened. By all accounts he was a complex and remarkable man of courage and determination having survived many storms on the oceans of the world. Through it all there must have been enough joy in the journey, as Tristan logged incredibly, some 450,000 miles on the oceans, many of those miles alone.

As a young teenager my first ride on a homemade motorbike was a very short ride ending with the bike on its side and its rider unhurt except for a scrape or two. In my early twenties, shadowed by that first experience I learned to ride a motorcycle. Galaxy 6 is not a sailboat journey on the high seas but a journey on the seat of a motorcycle. It is an account of a journey of Joy that through writing I have taken once again; "The Long Road Home."

A Distance Traveled
THE LONG ROAD HOME

It was a loop through the west-northwestern United States, a trip of 5,220 miles taken on a CX500 Honda Motorcycle. Packed in a knapsack were several changes of clothes, towels and personal belongings for hygiene and good health including a first-aid kit, sunblock, flashlight, a small transistor radio and a few other items. With the addition of a sketchpad (my journal), an atlas of the US, a Swiss style pocketknife and a camera, the knapsack was full. Packed in one of the duffle bags was a pup tent, Sterno fuel and a folding stove, matches and a lighter, a canteen set and a can-opener. Also stuffed inside was a winter coat that doubled as a pillow, a light rain suit, sweater, a windbreaker and gloves. I had with me an additional jacket that I generally wore when riding. A second duffle bag held my sleeping bag.

All of this I strapped to the carrier and backrest of the bike on the Sunday evening before my Monday morning departure. Along with my driver license and medical ID card, I carried on my person two-hundred dollars in Travelers Checks and twenty-five dollars in cash. I had no credit card or other cards of any consequence other than my banker's business card just in case the need for additional funds arose. Additionally I had a small zipper pack with a clear plastic map pocket strapped near the front of the gas tank for miscellaneous items and maps.

I was living at the home of two of my sisters in St. Paul, Minnesota and working in downtown St. Paul. I had arranged with my employer to take three weeks of time off.

I had volunteered to help as a counselor for persons with special needs who lived at Orvilla Group Home in Eagan, where I had recently worked for nearly a year. As a volunteer, I would accompany the van and would stay with the group of vacationers until Friday morning. The van would be leaving at 7:00am on Monday June 26, 1978. The Black Hills of South Dakota, a long day's ride would be the first leg of the trip.

Sunday evening after all that I needed was packed and strapped on the bike; I rode to the home of Gail and her son Scott. Gail worked as a counselor at Orvilla Group Home. Her place of residence was about a five-minute drive from Orvilla. This way I would not need to drive quite so far in the early morning and could sleep in about a half an hour longer. Gail and I visited about the upcoming week of camping with the Orvilla residents. Gail, her son Scott and another counselor would be traveling in the van with the residents who had signed up to vacation in the Black Hills. It was about 11:00pm when we decided we had better get some rest. I would sleep on the couch, assuring Gail I would be fine. I could not seem to get to sleep however. I turned one way and another. Often I would just lie on my back. I was not concerned about anything in particular but as the time passed, I began to have some concern about my alertness through the coming day. I had heard that even though a person may not sleep there is some benefit in the resting and that was at least some comfort. I thought about Charles Lindbergh and his difficulty in getting to sleep in the time before his solo flight across the Atlantic Ocean. It was sometime about 4:00am when at last I fell asleep only to be roused at 6:00am. Gail, Scott and I arrived at Orvilla about 6:30am and the van was packed, ready to go by 7:00am.

I did not have a set route once I left the Black Hills though the trip would take me on to Wyoming, the Bighorn Mountains, Ten Sleep Canyon, Yellowstone National Park and the Grand Tetons; then on into Idaho and Crater of the Moon National Monument and at last to Portland, Oregon and the Pacific Coast. From there I would travel into northern California and the Redwoods, and then back east over mountains, into the deserts and hot, dry lands of Nevada and Utah where stars filled the night skies, clear and bright, nearly down to the horizon. I would continue into Colorado and the Rockies, Nebraska, South Dakota and Minnesota and at last back home again to the Wisconsin family farm where my father, mother and two younger sisters, Lucy and Grace were living at the time.

I carried within me the gifts others had given me and those gifts sustained me in my daily travels. The experiences of the trip taught me the importance of facing my fears, trusting in my abilities, knowing my limits and understanding that goodness shown to others would in large measure mirror back to me through the goodness of the other.

Looking back it was, in some ways, a trip of blissful naivety filled with more risks than I was aware. It is no wonder my mother worried herself nearly sick. She later told me how she and dad would sit at the table after supper with maps spread out, wondering about the routes I may have taken and where I might be on a given night. There were no cell phones or GPS devices in 1978. Communication was far different than today. Mom also said that when she was anxious and worried, Dad counseled her not to worry so much. "There is nothing we can do but to trust in the Lord." I would like to think those evenings' Mom and Dad spent were full of memories and stories of their own lives together.

And so I continue with the excerpts and stories of a trip west I made on a motorcycle in the summer of 1978. The accounts of the ride are from a journal I kept, at least for a time, and from my memories of the trip.

1978
Monday, June 26th

Somehow, I had thought this day was my birthday, though I did not tell anybody. I felt fine even though I lay awake tossing and turning most of the night. I did finally get some sleep in the early morning hours. (*I would like to think lack of sleep was the cause of my confusion. Most people however would say, "It's just Bob.")* It was a nice day, with a good west wind. The bike has been working nicely and the engine is smooth with little vibration. Scott rode with me for about half the distance of today's twelve-hour drive. Scott is the son of Gail, one of two counselors working on the trip. My seat was sore nearing the end of the day but not so awful bad, I guess. We had left Orvilla Group Home at about 7:00am in the morning. The sun was just setting as we started up Rushmore Memorial Road with its famed hairpin turns.

The Black Hills are beautiful but I feel the chill in the night air with only a light insulated jacket on. My bike is also running on reserve fuel. Hope there's a gas station in these hills. The view of the hills from one of the hairpin turns is fantastic, the hills black against the blue of the mist. The drive up the mountain from Keystone is about nine miles. At last, we reach Rushmore Campground, our destination. The trip meter on the bike registers 620 miles – "Good grief!" We stop at the office and with our reservation confirmed set up camp. Everyone pitches in. A simple meal is prepared and we visit for a while. It has been a long day and everyone is tired and in bed by 11:30pm Mountain time. I slept great!

Tuesday, June 27th

I arose about 7:00am. I shared my tent space with Gene, one of the residents of Orvilla and he was still fast asleep in his sleeping bag. I exited through the flaps of the tent and a clear and beautiful morning gave greeting. I took the bike and then the van up for gas at the camp store. Filling out dates on the receipts I find out this day is my birthday, not the day before as I had thought. I told the group when I returned that it is my birthday and suddenly the hills were alive with the "sound of music" *(my apologies)* as they sang me a happy birthday.

I made a Malt-O-Meal breakfast for all. My seat is sore as I sit at the table for breakfast, so I stand and eat. At about 11:00am with everyone in the van and ready to go we were on our way for the day's tour. I started out driving the van and headed down the mountain along the winding road with its hairpin turns and short tunnels. *(As though designed as a preview — there is a beautiful view of Mount Rushmore in the distance framed by one of the tunnels on the Rushmore Memorial Road.)* We arrived at the Mount Rushmore Memorial and saw the four stone presidents up close and personal.

We then traveled to Flintstone Camp and ate lunch. Then it was on to Custer State Park. We traveled the Wild Life Loop in Custer. We saw two deer and a fawn. Four burros came up to the van and we saw them close up, as they began licking and slobbering the windows looking for handouts. Next, we went up the Needles Highway with its narrow roads and narrower tunnels. Finally, we arrived back at camp and fixed ham and beans for supper. Gene asked if he could have a ride on the back of my bike so I took him for a ride to Keystone and back again. We both enjoyed the ride of about twenty miles round trip. Back at camp, we all sat around the fire. Lying on my back for a moment, all of us gathered about the fire, I fell asleep. Gail or Scott woke me up as everyone was going to bed and I crawled into the tent for the night. I was tired. I slept really well.

Wednesday - Thursday, June 28th - 29th

No entries in the journal.

(As I recall everyone enjoyed their time in the Black Hills as we toured Rapid City and the Black Hills area. Thankfully all of us continued in good health.)

We visited Rapid City and Dinosaur Park on the 28th. Dinosaur Park was most memorable for what was said by one of the Orvilla residents, Gary I believe. It was something I would never in my life have thought about. As we walked under and around the life-size Brontosaurus, a huge, monstrous sculpture, I heard the comment "Their poop must have been big." As you might imagine there were a few laughs at that one.

Gene, one of the residents at Orvilla, asked to take a helicopter ride to view Mount Rushmore. It was required that one of the staff ride along. I waited for one of the two staff to volunteer but neither of the staff would go, so I, a bit reluctantly, volunteered. What a ride! Now that was flying, so like a bird. Gene and I both enjoyed the ride in the glass bubbled three passenger (including the pilot) whirlybird.

I took some time in the morning of one of the last two days in the hills to change the oil and the filter on the bike as a change would soon be due and it would be one less thing to think about as I went on my way west. Having filled the tank with gas a day or two ago the bike was good to go. The gas tank held something close to 5 gallons and at around 60 cents a gallon, a fill averaged about $2.50 or so depending on how much fuel remained in the tank at fill up.

There was time for relaxing, playing games and hiking the campground trails. We ate well and each night sat around the campfire telling stories. What more fun could one hope for? They were good people, each and every one. Such a blessing... I would miss them, however I did not yet know how much.

Friday, June 30th

I said my good-byes to all and left Mount Rushmore Campground at about 7:30am after packing, much of my things still damp with morning dew. *(At the time I had no idea whatsoever that I would someday return to this place some seven years later on a September honeymoon and again on two later visits with Barb and our first son David.)*

I enjoyed the ride in the cool of the morning air as I traveled to Rapid City. Once through Rapid City I turned onto I–90 heading west. This was open country with lots of room and warm. I stopped in Sundance, Wyoming for lunch. I had almost too much to eat for $2.57. The next stop was Gillette and finally Buffalo. Barely missed a prairie rainstorm between Gillette and Buffalo as I watched it skirt by. The smell of sagebrush as I traveled through Wyoming is wonderful. From Buffalo, I took the southern route of the Bighorn Mountains. *(I had first thought these mountains were the Rockies. Somehow, I was expecting to look out over the Pacific at the summit of the southern pass, though I knew there were more states to come.)*

The Bighorns were beautiful with fast running streams, clear blue lakes and wild flowers on grassy meadows and hillsides like I had never seen before. There was still some snow at the tops as I reached the summit of the pass.

Ten Sleep Canyon was gorgeous, quite a ride with lots of hairpin turns down and through its sheer, reddish walls. I stopped for gas in Ten Sleep. Whew, it's hot! I had put extra jackets on in the cool of the mountains and now took them off in the heat of Ten Sleep. I continued on to Worland through some desolate looking lands. This day I saw the first oil pumps in Wyoming. Worland is hot as are Manderson Basin, Greybull, all hot. Tired, hot, wind burned and thirsty I stopped in Greybull for something to eat and drink. Relaxing with a meal of chili and several glasses of water, I began to feel better. I decided to push on to Cody another hour or two away. It started to cool off between Greybull and Cody and with the sun getting low in the sky; I at last pulled into Cody, Wyoming at some time nearing 9:00pm. The sun was well behind the mountains to the west. I stopped at the first campground I came to and parked the bike.

I registered at the office, paid the tent camping fee of a few dollars, purchased some film for the camera, picked up a visitor's guide and walked back to the bike. I rode to the tent site not far from the office. The trip meter on the bike read 154 miles. It had read 715 when I left Rushmore Campground in the morning. Since the meter sets back to zero at 999, I calculated 439 miles traveled today.

My seat never really got sore though I felt tired and spent. I was beginning to have second thoughts about this trip. It is a darn lonely feeling, nobody to talk too really. I pitched my tent, with no other tents around, just big rig campers that seemed deserted of people. There was a rodeo nearby and I could hear the loudspeakers, announcers and the commotion. As I set camp, I gazed in the distance at bleachers of people and cars in large parking areas. I figured perhaps the number of people were in the thousands. I thought, 'That must be where everyone is tonight.'

I lay in the tent, and the troubling thought crossed my mind, 'I should just pack up my stuff and travel through the night heading east toward home.' I knew it would be a foolish and dangerous thing to do. I was tempted though, but my body told me I needed rest. I could head east in the morning if I so chose. I lay in my sleeping bag and continued with my thoughts, 'If I could only think of others rather than myself, perhaps I could let go of the awful feelings of isolation and fear I was experiencing that seemed to come out of nowhere.' I had just spent four nights with others in the Black Hills and I was dearly missing their company. I knew, as I had so often been reminded of by my mother, "molehills can grow into mountains when one is tired." I could hear the noise of the rodeo and all the people in the distance and yet I lay in the tent feeling so damned alone, and rather sorry for myself.

I began my prayers as I lay there and suddenly, 'Geez,' I thought, 'those poor missionaries new to foreign lands, not yet knowing the language or the people or those guys that sail the seas alone; I guess I got it made after all. I will say some prayers for them. I'll write some postcards in the morning and then maybe I won't feel quite so alone.' I began to wonder, 'Just how far I should travel on this trip west. No one would think the lesser of me if I just turned around now. No one would blame me for not making it to the Pacific. If it is no more than a thousand miles, I just might change my mind about heading back home, and continue on. Thoughts of failure, fear and anxiety about where I was and what I was doing had suddenly taken hold of me. I was exhausted. I soon fell asleep saying my prayers.

(Mom always told me, "Angels finish prayers when one falls asleep praying." ah, the wisdom of mothers!)

Saturday, July 1st

I awoke in the comfortable coolness of a new morning and heard what sounded like the engine of an older plane. I quickly unzipped the tent flaps and stuck my head out. I looked up to a bright blue sky just as a biplane came into sight over the pines of a wooded area to the south. My thoughts were the thoughts of a mind and body rejuvenated, simply by a good night's rest. 'What an adventure I am on and what a beautiful day.' These were my thoughts on a new and glorious morning.

I was refreshed, the fears of the night but a memory. How wonderful to be alive, to be in this place, in this moment, to ride and to experience country I have never seen before. I made a promise to myself that I would continue on to the Pacific, that I would make a commitment to embrace others with care and concern. I would be truly present to whomever I would meet on this "trip of a lifetime." A trip such as I may never take again. I would live each day as the gift it is. Once again, I now looked forward to Yellowstone Park and places west, yet unknown. Flipping through the pages of the Cody Visitor's Guide I decided to take some time on this morning and visit Cody's Whitney Museum of Western Art.

I showered, shaved and felt great, ready for the day. I packed up my belongings, swept out the sand from the tent, took it down and slid it into the duffle bag. The final process was strapping the knapsack and two duffle bags to the carrier and backrest. I mounted the bike and started the engine. I took the brochure from the small accessory pack strapped to the tank I looked at the map in the museum brochure one last time, while I listened to the bike and feathered the choke gradually to its running position. I returned the brochure to the pack confident of the route through town. The museum was not much more than a few miles and a few turns away, a piece of cake and this time it really was.

On the way to the art museum, I noticed a Catholic Church ahead and pulled over. St. Anthony of Padua was the name on the sign and I walked up to the rectory and gave a knock on the door. I waited a minute or so and just as I began, walking back to the bike the door opened. "Can I help you?" came the greeting. I replied, "I'm traveling to Yellowstone and am wondering if there are any churches in the park area." The priest informed me there is a mission church, St. Francis of Assisi in the park and gave me the information available. We had a pleasant conversation that lasted several minutes or so. I thanked him. He wished me a safe and enjoyable trip. As I left I thought, 'Yes, it really is all about people and being present to one another.' The struggles of last evening would be an unexpected blessing that would be with me in the days ahead.

The Whitney Museum of Western Art in Cody is a beautiful museum and I spent some time there. It was an interesting place featuring works by Albert Bierstadt, Charles M. Russell, N. C. Wyeth, Solon H. Borglum and other artists with paintings, bronze sculptures and many artifacts. The museum was also home to a collection of Winchester rifles and a Buffalo Bill Wild West exhibit. There was a Plains Indians exhibit and many other interesting areas all in one place, an impressive museum considering Cody's size.

Nearing lunchtime, I ate a sub sandwich, had a Coke and was soon on the road to Yellowstone's east park entrance.

The drive from Cody to the east entrance of Yellowstone National Park is about 50 miles. It was a spectacularly scenic ride and now just ahead, the 3,200 foot tunnel and the East Yellowstone Entrance.

What beautiful country, streams and mountains in the distance, peaks white with snow. It is big country. I am enjoying the views and vistas, stopping frequently along the way to really observe and take in all that surrounds me.

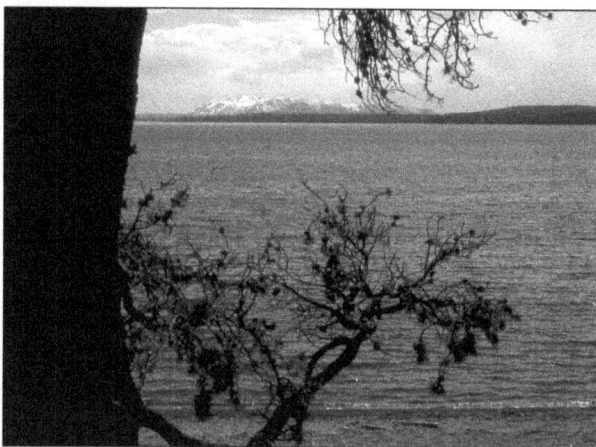

Arriving at the Fishing Village General Store I pulled up to the pumps for gas and purchased a can of soup and some fruit, my ordinary fare at the end of a day's ride. Here I met the Loons. They are from Idaho and traveling on a Yamaha 500, 'a nice bike' I thought. They asked if I had some chain lube oil. "Sorry, I don't have any as my bike is shaft driven," I replied. We visited a few minutes about bikes, trips, riding and such. Wishing one another safe travel, we parted ways. In our brief visit, they had suggested that I see the Grand Tetons just to the south of the park. I assured them that I certainly would. They waved as they rode away. I thought to myself, 'What a nice couple. The idea of being present to others, along with a smile, works wonders. This is a good way to live.'

I had seen a bear and a moose on my travel today as well as thermal springs and a falls on the Lewis River. A thundercloud skirted by as I left Yellowstone by way of the south entrance. I had thought to stay the night in Yellowstone but had found no place to camp.

I entered the Grand Tetons National Park and it is simply fantastic, indeed grand! The Tetons are beyond description, you really need to experience them in person. I close my eyes and still picture my first sighting of this magnificent range of mountains without foothills. They are truly a unique and beautiful range of mountains.

Riding along Jackson Lake I pulled into a wayside, parked the bike, and sat down along the shore for a while. I tuned in a station on the transistor radio and relaxed listening to music. I looked across Jackson Lake and the Teton peaks on the other side. What beauty lay before me, mountains soaring steeply upward to the sky, with snow-capped tops, even in July, reflected in the waters below. I thought, 'How very beautiful it all is. How wonderful it would be to sail these waters.' I was content however to sit for a while and dream.

The Commodores song "Three Times a Lady" started to play. I thought of Mary Jo, who I had recently started dating. 'How nice it would be if she could be here by my side.' It was not long and I was on the road heading south toward Jackson Hole.

I pulled over and stopped frequently as I traveled the park road that follows the Teton Mountain Range. It was now getting toward late afternoon as I pulled into the drive of the Sacred Heart Chapel and checked out the Mass times. There is a Mass scheduled in less than an hour. The Chapel built of logs is architecturally very pleasing. Not far from the Chapel's parking lot is a lake so I decide to relax, meditate, and just dream for a while at this beautiful spot. I had so much to thank God for, most importantly for the gift of life.

Soon a car arrived. I turned my head and a younger to middle age man got out of the car and by his attire, I figured he must be the priest who would celebrate the afternoon Mass. He walked over to where I was sitting and introduced himself, "Hi, I'm Father Hugh." I stood up introduced myself and we both sat down on the bank and visited perhaps ten minutes or so. He then excused himself, as he needed to make preparations and get things ready for the afternoon service.

In conversation, Father Hugh recommended that I take the Jenny Lake Loop Road, which loops around to the base of the mountains. "It would be well worth your time," he had said. I attended Mass and those about me participated well. It was good prayer. I thanked God for my safe travel and the many blessings of the past week. I left the Chapel and walked over to the bike. It was cooler now, the sun well behind the mountains. I took out a light jacket from the backpack, put it and my helmet on, started the bike and left the Chapel parking lot. I continued south toward Jackson in search of Jenny Lake Loop Road.

It was not long and there was a road sign, "Jenny Lake Loop Road." As I idled along the road I was aware, this was a place like no other. I could not help but think of Aunt Jenny, my Uncle Ralph's wife. She taught me to dance, rode in our chugs *(carts built by kids for riding down hills)* when we were young. Aunt Jenny was a kid at heart, and a beautiful, caring and fun loving woman.

Finally, I came upon the lake itself, a pristine, beautiful little lake with the highest banks on its western shore that I could ever have imagined. The camping spots on the southeast side of the lake disappointingly full. 'Darn-it,' was

all I could think, 'what a wonderful place this would have
been to pitch a tent and set up camp.' After some time soaking
up the beauty of this little lake and the magnificent mountain
I took leave of Jenny Lake, its beauty etched in memory.

I made my way to Teton Park Road and again headed
south. I stopped at a KOA just north of Jackson Hole. No
room, not even for a pup tent and a cycle. And so I continued
the search and found nothing available at any of the camps
in or near Jackson Hole. 'Poor Joseph and Mary looking for
an inn,' I thought. It takes some time, in stop and go traffic, to
travel the main street through town on a 4th of July weekend.
At last I turned west on a main east/west highway through
Jackson Hole and stopped at a Mobil station for gas. I asked
the attendant in the store if there might be any camping places
to stay for the night. He informed me about a primitive Forest
Service Camp along WY–22 Teton Pass Highway, a two-lane
road that winds up the mountain.

I got on the bike, snugged the straps of my helmet and started the engine, nudging the kickstand up I headed west and onto WY–22 with faith in what the attendant had said.

It is dark now as I continued the climb up the mountain road. I looked down into the darkness. Jackson is beautiful in the black of night with its glowing lights in the distance below as I traveled the road ever higher. Finally, I reached the crest of the 8,431 foot pass. And I then began an ever so gradual descent. I am in Targhee Forest. Just around a curve, I see the flickering of a campfire through the trees. I turn onto a road not sure if it is the camping area. The bike's headlight illuminating a sign ahead confirms that it is. It is a noisy place, not because of noisy people but from a wild mountain stream running through. I find an open spot and set up camp in the dark, as often is the case for me. I am so grateful to have a proper place to pitch a tent.

The stars are bright and beautiful! It is cold up here. I dig into my duffle bag and get out the Sterno, the folding stove and a can of soup. I heat the soup in the can placed directly on the Sterno stove inside the tent. I am careful to make sure that the stove is set within a metal plate and I leave the tent flaps open for good ventilation. It is not long and it's hot –"Soup this good just has to be Campbell's" and Campbell's Chunky Vegetable Beef Soup it was, a perfect spot for hot soup on a cold night nearly 8,400 feet above sea level. I ate the soup and had a fruit cup for dessert. It is after 11:00pm tired, I crawled into my sleeping bag, lay my head on my rolled up winter coat and was soon asleep. Not, however, until I worried for a brief time that the noise of the stream would keep me up.

Sunday, July 2nd

Woke up once during the night. Cold air is drafting down the back of my neck. I thought back to the farm and sleeping in a drafty upstairs bedroom of the farmhouse in Wisconsin on a cold of winter night. No problem. I wrap the sleeping bag snug around me and soon am back to sleep.

I awake and it is morning. I lie for a while in the cool tent and then finally crawl outside refreshed and ready for the day. It amazes me what sleep does for the body and mind. There in front of me is a spectacular snowcapped mountaintop that I assume is the Grand Teton of them all, gray rock and a field of snow beginning but a few hundred feet higher than where I stand. The stream is crazy wild with runoff.

A ways off a young man is walking and eating breakfast from a pan. As he comes closer we greet one another. His name is Wayne. In conversation I find out he too is a biker and touring alone, taking advantage of the long weekend. Noticing my bike, he mentioned that he worked for a Honda dealer in Cheney, Washington. He added, "Stop by and I'll tune the bike if you get to Cheney." In our visit, I also found out that the Honda CX500 recently won a prestigious race and bike award. "It's a good bike," he said. It was nice to hear knowing that 1978 was the first production year for the CX500 and I was just a bit apprehensive in the purchase of a first year model. Another fellow came over. His name was Bob Moore. We visited for quite some time. He was from Utah, on vacation with his family.

That morning I left camp with Wayne, as he too was heading west for a while. It was about 11:00am when we pulled into Idaho Falls and stopped at a Burger King. We ate lunch and traveled on to Arco and from there said our good-byes and went our separate ways. He turned heading north and I continued on west to Crater of the Moon National Monument.

It was along this road that I met a formation of some two dozen or so Harley motorcycles traveling east. I glanced as two by two they rumbled on by. Most of the riders were rather large guys, and all but two of them carried gals on the back seats of their bikes. Most of the gals sported short-shorts and halter-tops looking like poster pin-up models on their way to a photo shoot. I could not help thinking, 'Perhaps there is something more to a Harley man than I had thought.' Most of them waved, as is generally the custom when meeting bikers on the road. It was a most memorable Harley encounter, guys, gals, bikes and all.

Arriving at Crater of the Moon National Monument I parked the bike and strolled along the pathways. It was a unique area and I began to climb the highest hill in the area, Inferno Hill. Quite a climb and in the higher elevation I had to stop a time or two to catch my breath. It was quite a view from the top of that pile of black rubble. I strolled around the park paths for a while and then left. On my way out, I greeted a number of more mature couples on bikes just entering the park.

The landscape was quite interesting as I traveled from Crater of the Moon Monument to Mountain Lake, Idaho. It was rugged looking country. It was late afternoon when I got to a KOA camp just east of Boise. There I met Bob and his wife from somewhere north of Seattle. I also met Mr. McPherson, Mac from Portland, Oregon and Linda from Vancouver, Washington. After visiting awhile about riding and travel plans Mac asked if I would care to ride into Portland with him and Linda tomorrow. I was happy for the invitation and pleased to accept. I ate some grapes and heated a can of spaghetti for supper. I slept through the night. It was certainly much warmer here than Teton Pass where I had stayed the night before.

Monday, July 3rd

I was up early. The morning sky was gray and overcast. As I looked at the clouds, I wondered if today would be a day of rain. I began the morning ritual of getting things together, packing, disassembling the tent and the usual. Mac walked over and asked about a departure time. "I should be ready very soon," I said. "We're about ready as well," he replied.

Mac, Linda and I left the KOA camp at Boise about 7:45am. It was cool riding. We crossed the state line into Oregon and it was not long before the rain gave us our greeting. The rain here is different from the rain of the mid-west; the droplets are more like a mist. While not so harsh and stinging it is soaking. Due to the weather and road conditions, for the most part we do not do much side-by-side riding except for purposes of communication. I defer to Mac and take up the rear allowing plenty of room between us. Any emergency stop or maneuver on wet pavement is dicey and potentially catastrophic. I ride within my comfort zone and Mac adjusts his speed accordingly as well. As I ride, water collects on the seat between my legs, every so many miles I rise from the seat to allow the water to drain. After an hour or two we at last pull into a gas station.

The cold rain is taking a toll on me. The fingers on my hands are tingly and cold, I rub my hands together to bring back some of the warmth. By now my gloves are damp inside. Mac offers me the use of an extra storm jacket that he carried with him. It was certainly better than what I had. I wondered if perhaps he packed the extra jacket for some touring kid who had no clue of what an Oregon ride in the rain was like.

We are soon on our way again, same old, same old. Mac and Linda are up the road perhaps a quarter mile or so, quite a bit farther then our usual distance from one another. I increase my speed a bit to close the gap between us. At some point about that time the sudden appearance of a Jeep driving out of the long grass of the highway median startles me. Thankfully I am in the right lane and instinctively move from the left of the right lane to the right of the lane. The jeep remained in the left lane and soon sped out of sight. 'What had just happened,' I wondered. It seemed so bizarre. I thought of what could have been the consequences of that event and wondered if the driver even knew I was there. Thankfully it was same old after that.

Blue Mountain Pass is foggy and it continues to rain; if not for Mac and Linda I would have stopped many miles ago. We adjust speeds according to the densities of the fog and mist as we continue to ride. As we begin descending the mountain pass at long last we came out of the clouds. We soon stop at a restaurant along the highway, enjoy a nice dinner, and visit. Things are looking up again. About 200 miles still to go Mac informs me.

We are again back on the highway on a now pleasurable ride. Riding along ridges of high country I look down into the valleys below on fields green and beautiful in the light of the afternoon sun. I am actually pleasantly warm. Eventually the road descended following the sweeping high banks along the Columbia River. The wind is gusting, blowing strong out of the west. It was as if the wind was playing a game, testing our riding abilities, as one moment it was exceedingly strong and the next barely discernible. With the pavement dry, there was really no concern and I was rather enjoying the exercise and the lessons on the physics of balance, energy, action and reaction. Mac later told me the winds along the Columbia generally blow in from the east. Today had been different. Across the Columbia to my right were the green hillsides rising to blue skies over the state of Washington.

After what was a hard day's ride we pulled off the highway now within the city limits of Portland. We stopped along the side of the road. Mac invited me to stay for the night with them if I wished. I gladly accepted the kind offer and we rode to his home. In the time I had spent with them on the road and in our visits at stops along the way I found Mac and Linda to be good and caring people. I unloaded my belongings off the bike and carried them into the enclosed front porch, taking only the knapsack into the house. Mac showed me the guest room and I placed my knapsack on the floor next to the bed.

The house, a one-story structure with a living room, smaller kitchen, dining area, two bedrooms and a bath, I figure as probably built in the forties. It was modest, well-kept and comfortable. Mac invited me to make myself at home. I wrote out some postcards and asked Mac if I could make a long distance call to Wisconsin. "No problem" was the generous reply. I called Uncle Lawrence and Aunt Betty to let them know how things were going. Not wishing to make a second call, my aunt said she would be glad to call my folks for me.

Mac and Linda made waffles for supper, delicious. The both of them were most gracious and wonderful hosts. It took several hours for the effects of the ride on my body to subside, especially the warm tingly feeling on my face, arms and legs. I sat in one of the living room chairs and read a couple of magazine articles.

(I recall, almost photographically, reading an article in Readers Digest that evening, on healthy teeth. In the article, the author concluded that flossing is the most important things you can do for your dental health. I took that article to heart and floss daily, grateful for the article and my teeth.)

Tired from the day's ride I decided to go to bed a little earlier than usual. I slept in a real bed that night. What a treat.

Tuesday, July 4th

Linda made scrambled eggs, coffee and toast with jam for breakfast on this morning of the Fourth of July. It was for me a perfect breakfast. Mac gave me some directions and routes for some suggested touring. I left Mac and Linda's about 9:30am. I left most grateful for all they had done for me. I would like to think and believe I did leave a note of thanks with a few dollars to cover, at the very least, the cost of the phone call the night before; however it is not noted in the journal.

It was overcast and cool as I headed to Tillamook and the Pacific. I did not see Mount Hood on the morning of my departure from Portland due to the clouds as so often is the case. The road was winding, cut through the trees, a leisurely ride on a dry overcast morning. I had thought about traveling north into Washington state and to places like Seattle and Mount Rainier, northern Idaho, Glacier National Park, Montana and home. 'Perhaps I can do that route another time,' and that thought made my decision to head south an easier one to make. For now I would head south at least as far as the Redwood forests of California, perhaps as far south as San Francisco. From there I could head east to Nebraska and visit with some of my dad's relatives who I had come to know in their visits to Minnesota from time to time.

As I headed west the sky began to clear. I caught my first view of the Pacific through the clearing of some trees, a view that I only imagined days before as I traveled over the Bighorn Mountain range in Wyoming. I stopped for a while, contemplating the immense distance of ocean that lay before me. I had covered some 2,000 miles since leaving Minnesota, barely a fourth of the distance to many of the lands on the other side of the ocean before me. It was humbling to think of the immensity of the Pacific and of this world.

The sound of the surf is rhythmical and mesmerizing and the breezes blowing off the water, cool but refreshing. I had a lunch of some cherries and a can of tuna fish while relaxing, dreaming, wondering, gazing over the ocean and then looking back at the natural beauty of this stretch of northern Oregon coastline. I walk the beach for a while, feet in the mix of sand and ocean. After an hour or so I am back on the Oregon Coastline Highway 101. I travel losing track of time, the coast of Oregon so very beautiful. I stopped for an early supper and ordered a taco at a small establishment in Seal Rock about a third of the way down the coast. I got back on the cycle and rode a very short distance to nearby gas pumps and topped my tank and did some quick figuring; 66

mpg. Wow, best mileage I have had! I decided to turn inland to see what other kinds of scenery Oregon has to offer.

The drive inland was like the opening of a stage curtain and suddenly one is transported into another world. Wooded hillsides surround and meandering streams glisten in the late afternoon sun. Small farms with traditional houses, traditional barns and outbuildings dot the countryside, scenes pastoral and beautiful. The road winds through the valleys, following Beaver Creek, Elk Creek and others. Finally after what seems like a short trip, perhaps of a couple of hours, the quiet, country road I have been traveling intersects with Interstate 5. I head south toward California. *Oh to go back again.*

Nearing the time of sunset I exit and find a beautiful private camp just to the west of Roseburg, Oregon. The owner of the camp is sharp and witty. At the same time he seems to be ascertaining what sort of a person I am. Perhaps the fact I am on a Honda and not a Harley raised some questions. He looked over the registration slip I had just signed. "Buckner; any relation to General Buckner?" he asked. "Not that I know of," I replied and quickly added, "though my dad served in the Army in the South Pacific and I heard him mention of General Buckner a time or two." My dad had escorted officers to various places while serving in the Philippine Islands and Japan during WW II. The thought occurred to me, 'Perhaps General Buckner may have been one of the officers he escorted. I wondered.' "Follow me," he said. He hopped into the canopied golf cart, adorned with a half dozen or so smaller US flags, waving in the breeze. I quickly started the bike and followed. He directed me to an open area in the midst of large travel trailers and motor homes. I thanked my escort and began to unpack.

Two young girls came running over from a nearby trailer. They both introduced themselves, Melinda (the older) and Jennifer (the younger). They watched, moving with me as I set the tent, pushing stakes into the earth and setting the lines. As the setting of the tent neared completion their dad walked over and asked me if the girls were bothering me. "Oh, no, not at all," replied, "I grew up with lots of sisters and brothers. I have a younger sister Grace just a few years older than Melinda." We introduced ourselves, his name was Gary Berg from Seattle, Washington and his wife's name was Judy. I then began to start a fire and finally with a little help from my new neighbors it was burning nicely.

Gary left with the girls in hand and I sat down to relax and do some writing in my journal. A little while later Gary and Judy came over to the campfire. I stopped writing and tossed my journal in the tent. Gary introduced me to his wife, I welcomed them to sit down on one of the benches, and so we began to visit. Another couple came over, introduced themselves and joined us. They were Don Larson from Pacific, California and his friend Dianne.

Don was retired having served twenty years in the Army and worked as a metal plater. He looked over my bike and filled me in with regard to the metal alloys that made up the various parts of the bike's wheels. He seemed a very interesting kind of guy with a creative and inquisitive sort of mind. Later on, as the evening visit continued he mentioned that he had become quite proficient at handwriting analysis through the years and he related some interesting stories to us. He originally learned handwriting analysis from a Catholic nun who taught him while he was in grade school. It is amazing what the nuns know.

"Write your names," he said. "I'll give an analysis of what sort of person you are by analyzing your signatures." It seemed a bit intimidating but at the same time I was curious as to what he might know about me, without really knowing me. Gary, Judy and I wrote our names. His analysis proved to be most interesting and remarkably accurate about the sort of person I perceived myself to be. Suffice it to say it was a most interesting exercise. I do not remember what he said with regard to the signatures of Gary or Judy. It was all very fun as well as an icebreaker and we continued visiting until sometime about midnight. We said our good-byes and before leaving, Don gave me directions for finding the Redwoods. I thanked him for the directions. I had no real idea where they were exactly and now, thanks to Don I did.

The fire, now but glowing red embers, burned within the fire ring. I sat for a while longer enjoying the peace of the night, the present moment. I had assumed early on that this camp might be a bit stuffy but it turned out to be wonderfully "real"– what an enjoyable evening this had been. I then crawled into the tent, head on my coat I was soon asleep.

Wednesday, July 5th

I awoke about 7:30am. dressed and was out of the tent by 8:00am. Soon Melinda and Jennifer came over and I wished them a good morning. I gave them each a job to do and they helped me take down my tent. As I continued to pack Gary came over and invited me to come over for a breakfast of pancakes and plums. "Thanks" I said, "I'll be over in a few minutes," I replied. 'It was nice of them to invite me over,' I thought. The girl's tasks completed they returned to the trailer with their dad. I finished packing everything and strapped it all in place. I then walked over to their trailer.

Judy opened the screen door and I was welcomed in. Everything smelled and tasted so good, delicious in its pure simplicity. We visited and I so enjoyed the spirit and goodness of this young family. It was for me a memorable breakfast. Judy informed me the girls were up early. The first thing they asked, "Is he still here mom?" She said the girls had never got up that early on the trip before. 'Ah, shucks,' I thought. At about 9:30am I said good-bye to the Bergs and to Don and Dianne who were by now up and relaxing in chairs alongside their trailer.

I headed south on Interstate 5 toward Grant's Pass and then on to Crescent City, California. I reflected on my stay in Roseburg, Oregon. The "Rose" was an apt name indeed. The ride was very nice, the day bright and beautiful. The California border is regulated and the road divided into several lanes as I neared the border crossing. There were border officials checking for any produce that might be coming into California. By the questioning I received, plant disease and anything carried into the state that might endanger or affect field and flora was about all that was of interest. I had no fresh fruits, vegetables or plants and the woman working the security booth welcomed me to California wishing me a safe travel and pleasant visit.

Just before Crescent City I see my first redwoods. I can hardly believe how big they are. It is unlike anything I have ever experienced. This forest is like a fairyland, so beautiful, and all that enters so very small! Even the RVs, 5th wheelers and semi-trucks look small. I stop and just stroll for a while among these awesome giants. Huge ferns, though dwarfed by the trees, surround me. The carpet of fallen needles and debris, a cushion of decay under my feet, all of it so different from any forest I have ever experienced. I look upwards into the branches and needles so far above the earth. I see small patches of blue and sunlight filtering through. 'I'll take some more pictures in the "Valley of the Giants" later,' I thought to myself as I clicked the camera shutter a couple of times. As it turned out this grove of redwoods would be the only redwoods I would see on this trip.

The coastline of California somehow did not leave much of an impression on me as I traveled down Highway 101. I hit a stretch of road under construction. It was a delay of about a half hour. I was beginning to get just a bit tired and hungry as I enter the city limits of Eureka, a relatively large city. It seemed nothing special, just another busy city and I came west to get away from big cities. I usually enjoy KFC and having spotted one ahead stopped to eat. I ordered a meal and not impressed by the food received. It was a good price to pay and the pieces of chicken seemed small. Perhaps the redwoods somehow altered my sense of scale. The meal was somewhat bland I thought as well, not as expected. Someone must have forgotten one of the Colonel's secret ingredients. I left Eureka heading south and some miles down the road, I decided I had enough. The traffic south of Eureka had seemed to intensify with every mile south. I do not want to mess with the traffic that I was sure would get worse as I traveled south. So, turning around I backtracked north to Arcata and turned inland into the Salmon Mountains.

The drive east of Arcata is quite beautiful; I am pleased with my decision. I am out of the redwoods now and never did get a good picture of the big trees. I was not even sure how I would have gotten a good picture, as their scale is so immense. 'Oh well, some other time,' I thought. I finally arrived at a camp area just east of Salyer. The people who own the camp are very nice. A woman, one of the owners, showed me how to pan for gold, just in case I ever decide to try. I set up camp, washed my clothes in the camp laundry facility and then joined in some volleyball play with a couple of young women who introduced themselves as daughters of the camp's owners. A guy named Jack and some other kids were playing.

When the volleyball games finished I went back to my tent site and heated a can of soup, ate some plums and an apple that I had purchased when I had stopped for gas somewhere near Eureka and that was my supper. Later I met the couple next to my campsite, Ken and Ann from the state of Washington. We sat and visited until about 11:00pm or so. In casual conversation I found they had forgotten to pack towels. I borrowed them a towel, just freshly washed and dried to use for their showers in the morning. The two of them have no tent and are sleeping under the stars.

(July 5 was the last dated entry I made in the journal—most of the writing up to now is from the journal, with edits and additional material added. The following day-to-day account of the remainder of the trip is from memory as I traveled back in time some 33 years ago. I close my eyes and it is almost as though time never carried forward. What wondrous gifts we are within our being, within our memories, within all that we are.)

Thursday, July 6th

The early morning of July 6th was clear and the air heavy with dew. I noticed Ken and Ann still in their sleeping bags wet with dew. I set off for the showers, enjoyed a nice warm shower, and made my way back to the tent. The tent fly was still damp with dew. Ken and Ann are up now, their bags draped on the picnic table. They have apparently made their way to the showers. I began to pack my belongings. As I prepared to leave, Ken and Ann returned and handed me the towel, thanking me, apologized for its dampness. "You're welcome, glad to help out" I replied. I place it in the duffle bag since the tent, and the fly was still a bit damp as well. In the heat of the day and the breeze of a moving bike all will soon be dry. With everything strapped to the bike, I was set to leave. I said good-bye to Ken and Ann, wished them both well and headed east.

My stay at the campground in Salyer was most pleasant. The morning is bright and beautiful. I am traveling Highway 299 through the foothills and mountains of northern California. The road is winding with lots of ups and downs, an enjoyable road to travel on a motorcycle. Now and then as the road climbs I catch sight of a range of snowcapped mountains, beautiful in the light of this day. As I recall the ride that day for the most part was very scenic, taking me through Redding, and eventually connecting with Highway 395 heading south and east to Susanville. I begin seeing signs along the highway advertising Lake Tahoe. I am tempted as I had heard nothing but rave reviews about the area. I decide however to continue on to Reno as my funds and time away were close to the halfway point. Perhaps I will get to see Tahoe another time.

I cross the border into Nevada and Reno is getting close. The temperature is quite warm. Arriving in Reno I pull into a gas station and fill the tank. I thought of taking $5 or $10 and trying my luck with some gambling but I have second thoughts. I might need most, if not all of what money reserves I have left to get home. I never pulled the arm of a slot machine.

I left Reno and continued on I–80 toward Salt Lake City. Salt Lake City is somewhat north of where I wanted to be so when I reached the city of Fernley I made the decision to take a more southeastern route. I headed to Fallon having connected with Highway 50. It is nearing sunset. Just outside of Fallon there is a bar and restaurant so I stop for a soda and some water. I asked one of the patrons what the high temperature was for the day, as it had seemed quite warm. If I recall correctly "117 degrees" was the answer given. It was hot. I decide it might be prudent to put some of this desert heat behind me and travel into the night at least for a few hours. I started east on 50 and a sign reads, "Next Services 121 miles." 'A lot of nothing,' I thought.

A tabletop of desert, rimmed by the dark silhouette of butte formations, typical of many areas of the western landscape, surrounds me. Traveling in the cool of the night, through the desert east of Fallon, I am in awe of the night skies and the vivid clarity and multitudes of stars shining in the deep, even to the horizon before me.

There is nothing but the occasional "Caution, Free Range Cattle" signs and several signs marking restricted, forbidden lands. The windscreen of the bike helps to deflect some of the rush of cold air. Wearing a sweater under a winter jacket and gloves on my hands, I am reasonably comfortable. I am alone. Suddenly an uncomfortable thought comes to mind, 'What if my cycle decides to quit?' For a brief moment, I grasp the reality of where I am and give the side of the gas tank a pat, "Don't fail me now!" I spoke aloud as if the bike had ears to hear me. I touch quickly the left side valve cover; 'warm, smooth, everything is fine.' I continue the ride into the night.

It seemed rather weird to me that it could get so hot during the day and cool down to temperatures that I estimated to be somewhere in the 50–60 degree range, based on my riding experience and what I was wearing to stay comfortable. I pulled to the side of the road a couple of times just to look at a sky so full of stars. I met several groups of 2–3 vehicles. That was about all I remember of the traffic. I never saw headlights behind or taillights ahead on the entire stretch of road.

As I pulled into the small town of Austin it was nearing 11:00pm. I stopped at the only convenience store with gas pumps that I found still open. I topped the tank and went inside. I did not want to run out of gas in country such as this. I asked how late they were open as I selected a couple of candy bars. "Eleven" replied the attendant. I asked if he knew of a place to camp for the night. "There is a Forest Service Camp at the top of the mountain just east of here," he answered. I paid for the gas and candy bars and left the store. I got on the bike grateful for a topped tank of gas and soon began winding the way up the mountain.

A semi ahead was climbing slowly up the road. I had noticed the semi roll by as I was filling my tank at the gas pumps. Due to the constant curving road along walls of rock it was nearly impossible to pass safely. I was not in any hurry, so I patiently followed.

The smell of the diesel exhaust of trucks climbing hills is unpleasant and irritating. I had experienced it in northern California's mountain drives as I followed trucks hauling huge redwood trunks. After fifteen to twenty minutes of following one of them I would begin to feel slightly ill.

On my route in northern California there were entire hills full of trees that had been "clear cut," with nothing but stumps remaining. I wondered at the wisdom. *(It would be interesting after all this time to see those same hills and what they might look like today, some 33 years later. I hope some of the scars have healed.)*

At some point the truck pulled over at a wayside and parked, turning off its lights. I had passed a couple of parked semis on this night ride through desert only an hour or two before. I assumed they were getting some needed sleep, as I assumed the driver of this rig was about to do. It was not long and I reached the crest of the hill. A mile or so further I noticed a sign and dirt road. At last, the Forest

Service Camp and some needed rest. 'Good deal,' I thought to myself, 'at last a place to sleep for the night.'

It was just about midnight now, I set up the tent in the dimness of the night and tossing my belongings in the tent crawled into the sleeping bag and soon fell asleep. I was tired. It had been a hot and long day's riding that stretched well into the night. As I lay there I heard the unmistakable sound of a Harley driving up the entrance road and around the circle. Perhaps whoever it was already had a tent set up or was about to set one now. I drifted off to sleep.

Friday, July 7th

The tent warms quickly with the sun's rising. I awoke and stepped outside the tent. I looked out over the valley below. Smaller evergreens, looking more like shrubs than trees dotted the valley, 'a National Forest?' I thought, 'hmm, in Minnesota it would not come close to qualifying as a forest.' But then this is Nevada and all things are relative. Trees are rare and precious here. I was pleased that these trees were set aside and protected. Though scrubby, perhaps they were older than many of the larger trees back home.

I packed up and was soon on my way headed east. I do not recall where I stopped for brunch this day, though I probably did at some point. It was a part of my daily routine. I remember the day was heating up fast. The place I had camped last night was about the midway point, at the latitude I was traveling, from Nevada's western border to the eastern border of its neighboring state, Utah. I would cross the state line into Utah I estimated sometime about noon or so if all went well.

Once down the mountain the terrain was again rather flat and desert-like. I was pleased that my bike was liquid cooled and as such the engine heat minimal. I could pat the valve covers and hold my hand for a few moments without the danger of burning them as would happen almost instantaneously with an air-cooled engine.

Utah's landscape initially was much the same as Nevada's with its desert-like lands, though I noticed more and more large red rock formations as I traveled into the heart of the state.

I recall few if any speed limit signs in Utah or Nevada. I generally traveled no more than 65 to 75 miles per hour on relatively straight roads often for many miles. I remember one stretch of land for the most part flat. Traveling on a road that was a mix of straightaways and gentle curves, I was traveling about 70 mph at the time and noticed a group of cars quite a distance away in my rearview mirrors. There were few vehicles on this road. I met perhaps a dozen or so cars and trucks in an hour's time, usually two or three to a group it seemed. I had actually begun to wonder if this was for reasons of safety that vehicles traveled in clusters rather than singly. The cars in the mirror were fast approaching. I figured they were doing perhaps 90 mph and probably more. One by one they passed me; all were various models and years of Porsches. It must have been a car club enjoying a day's drive. As the last car passed I accelerated to 90 mph or so, and the cars were gradually disappearing out of sight. I throttled back to a more leisurely 65–70 mph enjoying the ride.

There is little forgiveness on a motorcycle. If for some reason a tire suddenly goes flat at moderate speeds, there is a chance of escaping serious injury. In my experience a sudden flat tire is not a good feeling at 60 mph however!

(Several years later I experienced a sudden loss of air in a rear tire at 60 mph during rush hour traffic. I figure I was lucky to come to an ever so gradual stop on the left shoulder of the highway as I had been traveling in the left lane. It was as if I was suddenly riding Gumby's horse Pokey, as the frame felt as if it had turned from metal into rubber. I pushed the bike more to the center of the median. I then waited perhaps five or so minutes for an opening safe enough to cross to the other side and go for assistance.)

I rode day after day, the sun and wind in my face. Every day I smeared the creamy white sunblock liberally on my face and any exposed skin. I can only imagine what I would have looked like had I not done so on a regular basis. The rush of wind and the heat felt like a blast furnace as I traveled this hot and arid land. Some of the scenery was quite extraordinary, reminiscent of scenes from Hollywood Westerns. Though picturesque, it never occurred to me what an extreme environment this country really is.

It was about mid-afternoon and as I approached a town in Utah I passed by some irrigated fields along the highway. The cool I felt was but a few moments of heaven! I stopped along the highway just to enjoy the cool for a few minutes.

Highway 50 merged with I–70. It had been a scenic day of riding though it had been hot. I decided to make camp at a KOA in Green River, Utah. The shower felt great after two days riding since having my last shower in Salyer. My usual ritual was a primitive camp one night and a camp with amenities the next.

Though I could not recall where I stopped for lunch or brunch on this day, I do recall I roasted a couple of brats purchased at the camp store on this evening. The camp was a rather nice camp and I enjoyed the campfire and an evening alone on this night.

(There is a note in the journal for July 7 of a trip meter reading of 275–755 or 480 miles.)

Saturday, July 8th

I left Green River shortly after sunrise. I was on the road at about 7:30am headed east on I–70. Grand Junction Colorado was less than a two-hour ride away, and home to Floss, a life-long friend of my mother. As I traveled by Grand Junction I thought of her. I did not have her phone number or address with me nor could I remember her last name so I continued on, looking forward to the cool of the mountains.

Sometime about 11:00am I came to the town of New Castle. My preference for dining on my travels was, and still is, to look for local "mom and pop" restaurants. I spotted a restaurant on the north side of the highway. There were a number of cars in the parking area, generally a good sign and so I exited, parked the bike in the lot and went inside for some brunch. I sat at a table near the window facing south. I looked out at tree-covered hills. It was always nice to relax and take a break from riding. Riding is more physical and mental than one might imagine. Mile after mile can become far more work than play. I was glad to be traveling in the more temperate climate of the higher elevations now. What a refreshing change from the plains and desert-like heat of the last couple of days.

A waiter came with water and a menu. After some introductory chatting I found out that he was from the northeastern United States, Vermont or Connecticut, as I recall. He had left in early summer on his own solo motorcycle trip to the west and Pacific coast. This too, was his first trip west. He mentioned that unfortunately his bike had broken down near New Castle. The transmission on his Harley gave out. He found a motorcycle repair shop nearby. The repair would be an expensive one, costing more than he would be able to pay. Thankfully, the owner of the restaurant offered him a job as a waiter and he was working to pay for the repairs to his bike and have a little additional money to live on while he waited out the days. He had paid for the parts and they were now on order. He figured he would be on his way home in a week or two when the parts arrived and the mechanic made the repairs.

He seemed like a fine young man, very personable and considering his circumstances, seemed to be taking things in stride. He certainly was doing a good job as a waiter. I observed his interaction with other patrons of the restaurant, he seemed to me a good hire and I imagined the proprietor of the restaurant would miss him when he left for home.

The waiter soon arrived with my order. "Is there anything else I can get you?" he asked. "Looks good," I replied. I enjoyed brunch, usually ordered from the breakfast menu, eggs or an omelet, bacon and/or sausage, potatoes and a glass of juice. I was not yet into coffee, I could take it or leave it at this time of my life and I would usually leave it. I finished what was a very nice breakfast and left a good tip on the table, paid for the meal and wished the waiter a safe trip home.

I continued east into the Rockies. Colorado and the mountains were all new to me, every mile truly a feast for the eyes. The majesty of the mountains and pastoral vistas of valleys below were here in abundance. Ah, John Denver, now at last I could more fully understand and appreciate the music and lyrics written with your heart and soul.

The road to Estes Park closed as I recall because of a recent snow. Its closure due to snow in the height of the summer seemed odd to me. These mountains were better than 14,000 ft. and the passes high so perhaps there well could have been some significant snow in the park. I had looked forward to seeing the park as I heard from friends it was a beautiful park. It was just a bit disappointed having to take an alternate route.

I skirted the city of Denver as best I could and headed for the plains and Nebraska. Traveling I–76 in the late afternoon, east-northeast of Denver I was already missing the incredible beauty of the Rocky Mountains.

I stopped for the evening at Fort Morgan, Colorado and located a campground on the Jackson Lake Reservoir. I pitched my tent in an area reserved for tenting. There were, as was usual, lots of RVs and very few tents. I set up camp and relaxed. Again, the evening meal I enjoyed that night was a mystery though I most always had something to eat. The brunch I had in New Castle earlier today had sustained me through the day. I often found something good to snack on at the gas stops I made every 200 miles or so.

I strolled along the banks of the reservoir and met a middle-aged couple out for a stroll as well. They introduced themselves as Robert and Ester Schott of Fort Morgan, Colorado. We visited a while on the path along the western shore of the reservoir enjoying the setting of the sun and the close of the day.

It was a beautiful night at the Jackson Lake Reservoir. I looked up at the stars in the night sky and contemplated the immensity and mystery of it all. I crawled into the tent and was soon fast asleep.

Sunday, July 9th

Suddenly in the mix of slumber and wakefulness I heard a loud cracking sound and opened my eyes to blackness and the realization that the tent had collapsed on me. The wind blowing across the flatland prairie was strong and gusty.

Groping in the dark, I at last found the zipper, unzipped the flaps, and made my way outside. The tent stakes were pulled from the soil that was probably about 80 percent sand with 20 percent humus; just the right mix of soil to sustain the poor, spotty grasses and vegetation that covered the area.

'It must be several hours until sunrise,' I thought. I dug around in the ground to find firmer soil in which to stake the tent lines. The wind is strong from the west. I am not sure how long the newly positioned stakes will hold but for now, they seem to be holding. I crawl back into the tent thinking it was a good thing the backpack and duffle bag were inside holding the tent down or I may have had a tent sailing across the waters of Jackson Lake Reservoir. I lie there for a while listening to the wind and ripple of the fabric and soon fell asleep a second time.

Again, as before, I awoke to the sound of the snapping and the beating of the tent on me. I again unzip the flaps and crawl outside. This time I shift the tent over and look for some rocks or something that I could use to lodge the stakes into the very sandy soil. OK! This is getting to be a bit of a nuisance but I will give it one more try. A third time I am hoping is the charm. I look up at the starry sky. I suppose the stars are laughing by now as well as anyone else who might be watching. Again I crawl in and again I fall asleep listening to the incessant wind. And again it is "ground hog day" as the tent has collapsed for the third time. By this time it is almost amusing. I unzip the flaps, crawl outside, this time dragging my sleeping bag with me. OK wind, I give and you win so I lay in the sleeping bag on top of the tent for a while. The eastern horizon across Jackson Lake Reservoir is beginning to brighten. I lay there for a time and am no longer able to fall asleep I start packing.

As I packed the last of my stuff on the back of the motorcycle I started walking down the road to the men's room. A man in a trailer nearby my site offered me a cup of coffee and a roll on my return. "Thank you, that would be nice," I replied, in a subdued tone of voice, aware that most people were still sleeping. I soon returned and we introduced our-selves to one another. Jack Hienrich of West Minister, Colo-rado invited me into his trailer. I sat down at the dining table and he poured a cup of coffee. 'I guess there are some advan-tages to these bigger rigs,' I thought. Though I was not an everyday drinker of coffee at the time it was a nice hot cup of coffee and I enjoyed it along with the roll. We visited for quite a while and I shared with him the story of my night. Perhaps my host appreciated the company as much as I did the coffee and roll. What a great way to start the day! By now the dim light of early morning had brightened into day. I thanked Jack for the visit and the good start to the morning and left the trailer.

All packed and ready to go I turned the key ignition on, toed the gear into neutral, opened the gas line and pulled the choke full. I pushed the starter button and the engine came to life. I sat relaxed, snugging the straps on my helmet as I waited for the rpms to build. I then feathered the choke gradually to the close position. With the rpms just above 700, I squeezed the clutch, pressed the gear into first, released the clutch and puttered down the roadway. I hoped the engine was quiet enough so as not to disturb those guests sleeping on this still early morning.

I was soon back on I–80 on my way to a farm near a small town of Madrid, Nebraska, about 35 miles south-southeast of Ogallala. The city of Ogallala is along I–80 and about 25 miles east of the lower southwest Colorado–Nebraska bor-der. I headed for the Hanson farm near Madrid.

I met Ed Hanson, a cousin of my father's, and Virginia, his wife for the first time only a year or two prior to this my first visit to Nebraska. They had come to visit my dad, and Dad's mom, Grandma Cora who lived about 15 miles from my par-ent's farm in Amery, Wisconsin. They visited my parents at the farm and met a few other relatives during their stay. As I recall Ed and Virginia were newlyweds at that time both in their second marriage. In various visits, Duluth and Superior was the subject of conversation. And so I volunteered to take

Ed, Virginia and Grandma Cora on a day trip to Duluth and the North Shore of Lake Superior in Minnesota.

Ed loved desserts and pie was his favorite. My mother having learned about Ed's penchant for pie baked some very special pies for Ed and Virginia. They were some of my mother's best and Ed, quite selflessly shared pieces of pie as he gathered with others.

The North Shore Drive is beautiful, known for scenic overlooks, parks and so much more. As we traveled along the thought occurred to me 'Ed might enjoy a piece of Betty's pie.' A few miles down the road, I pulled into the parking lot at Betty's Pies. Ed raved about the pie on a number of occasions on that day, the next and the next.

Ed, surprised by how many county and town roads in Minnesota and Wisconsin are paved remarked, "Most roads in Nebraska are dirt." Ed also figured my dad must have had some influence with the county to have a paved road up to his place. At the time of their visit, a freshly paved road ended at the north property line of the farm. Who knows, maybe Ed was right?

I exited I–80 onto a county road that took me south to Madrid. Ed was right; most of the roads here were of dirt but relatively smooth going. It was sometime about noon as I turned into the driveway of their farm southwest of Madrid, Nebraska. A small pond with ducks, geese and other farm animals were there to greet me. It was good to see Ed and Virginia again.

Monday - Tuesday - Wednesday,
July 10th - 11th - 12th

A diesel motor runs all through the night, pumping water for the irrigation of the fields. I lay on a bed in the upper guest room of Ed and Virginia's simple farmhouse amid the flatland fields of wheat and a variety of other crops. Wheat is a major crop and this time of year, the fields needed the moisture to ensure a good harvest.

How nice it was to sleep in a bed again. It had been a week ago in Portland that I last had the luxury. I listened to the steady drone of the engine in the distance through the open window of the bedroom and was soon fast asleep.

I had not planned on an extended stay at the home of Ed and Virginia, it just happened that way. It is strange to me now but I do not remember much of my time there. I do remember helping to feed some of the farm animals including the pigs. I walked the fields and entered into the experience of life on a Nebraska farm. Wheat farming was something I knew little about. I remember visiting with Ed about farming on quite a number of occasions.

I remember one of our conversations related to irrigation and the rules and regulations designed to help protect the aquifers. Unfortunately some of the aquifers were in decline and since water is so important to the health and yield of the crops it was of concern to Ed as well as all the area farmers. I sensed Ed was concerned for the future of farming. Changes are in the works so that water tables will remain at healthy levels. Without water their way of life would be no more.

I enjoyed the meals and visits we had at the dinner table. My stay was comfortable and in my time with Ed and Virginia I never wanted for anything. They were gracious hosts.

I went to the town of Madrid a couple of times. Madrid has a main street and a few side streets. It is a typical rural town with grain bins, a rail line, schools, churches, local businesses and homes. Surrounding the town, nothing but fields and farms as far as the eye can see.

One of the highlights of my time with Ed and Virginia was a trip to the city of Ogallala. Just north of the city is one of the largest earthen dams in the United States. This dam forms Lake McConaughy on the North Platte River. We stood for a while and gazed over the lake on the west side of the dam. The lake that formed was miles wide and many miles in length.

To the east was the winding North Platte River. Ed was well aware of the difficulties of managing precious water resources and the headaches involved in providing habitat for wildlife as well as the needed water for farm fields. Farmers for miles along the river depend on the North Platte for the irrigation of crops in a semi-arid land.

Thursday, July 13th

I most always find the good-byes difficult but it is always in the mix of life. I said good-bye to Ed and Virginia Hanson. We had discussed the route to Ed's Cousin Jim Hanson's place and Daisy's, an aunt to Ed. I traveled to Jim's cattle ranch, not far from the home of Daisy, mother to Jim and Dick. I had never met Jim but knowing Daisy, his brother Dick and Cousin

Ed, I was looking forward to meeting him. The route took me eastward and to the north of the interstate. It was sometime in the afternoon when I pulled into the drive of Jim's ranch.

Jim working outside came over to meet me. Introducing ourselves, we shook hands. Jim raised beef cattle and had a sizable operation. I do not recall how many head of cattle he cared for but it was well into the hundreds.

Jim had bought a cattle operation in Missouri some years before, in addition to his Nebraska ranch, but had sold it and moved back to the Nebraska ranch. We walked around, looked out over the land, and visited for quite a spell. I enjoyed the conversation and time spent with Jim. The business aspect of ranching amazes me and the financial resources involved in raising beef cattle are a tidy sum. It was again an aspect of farming I did not know. Jim mentioned in our conversation that he was paying interest on a million dollars in loans. 'Wow.' I thought but it takes money for machines, tractors, trucks, and so much more to keep a farm operating.

We visited about his mother Daisy and other things as related to family and kin. Daisy lived just a few miles down the road from Jim's ranch. Jim checked in on Daisy regularly and took her to town when necessary. As I recall Daisy no longer drove, perhaps she never did. I really do not know.

I left Jim's place and headed for Daisy's home. As I travel down the road, a crop duster flies low over fields ahead. I decide to stop and watch for a while. How low to the ground the pilot flew. As the plane neared the edge of the field, the pilot pulled the plane up and over the wires and making a turn, came in low clearing the wires and was again spraying the next swath of land and so it went. I watched from a safe distance as the process repeated again and again. These were large fields. As the plane made yet another turn and headed down the field, I started the bike and continued down the road, anxious to see Daisy again. I was to spend the night at her home. It had been quite a few years since I had last seen Daisy. I looked forward to seeing her once again, to enjoy her company, the vibrancy of her spirit and good nature.

Daisy welcomed me that afternoon with open arms. What a joy it was to see her once again. The guest room was ready and I carried my knapsack and belongings inside. Daisy continued, busily preparing the evening meal. We visited as she continued with the meal preparation.

As I recall, Jim joined Daisy and I for dinner that late afternoon or early evening. I shared my experience of watching the crop dusting plane. Jim spoke about what a dangerous job crop dusting was and talked about recent mishaps in the area, the injuries suffered and if I remember correctly, the death of one of the crop dusters a few years before.

I enjoyed the further visits with Jim, getting to know just a little more about the life of my extended family. After a time, Jim said his goodbyes and headed home. Relaxing in comfortable chairs Daisy and I visited about anything and everything. Her time in Nebraska spanned many years and her life was a treasure of memories. Daisy's was a life lived on the prairies of Nebraska living at a time when sod homes dotted the prairies and were the norm of the architecture of a prairie home.

Friday, July 14th

As I awoke the glow of red light filled the room as if the sun itself had entered within. The Nebraska prairie I thought was on fire. Quickly I dressed and left the room, expecting heat and confusion, but the house was peaceful and cool. I opened the front door and stepped outside. Expecting the heat of a searing fire, a cool mist of a Nebraska morning was my greeting. It was as if both panic and peace were my gifts of this morning. It was a startling experience.

I walked to the edge of the lawn. A field of corn, wet and drenched with morning dew, young stalks of early summer with broad curling leaves arched their way across the plowed earth of the prairie. The eastern sky was ablaze and a thousand rainbows surrounded me. The motorcycle that had carried me across desert and over mountains to this place on the prairie sat parked in the yard. Painted with the reflected light of this morning it appeared as if it were a photograph found in a biker magazine.

I remember Daisy so very well, her and grandma, my dad's mom, sharing with one another lives rich with memories. Having met Daisy only a few times as a young man, she had made an indelible impression on my heart. After a short stroll and a few moments thought and recollection on this memorable morning sunrise, I went back into the house. Daisy was up and greeted me with a hearty, "Good morning." Her voice and manner was as if she had been the study of "Minnie Pearl" whose stage persona endeared her to the hearts of so many people.

Daisy, aunt to my dad and sister-in-law to my grandma, was a strong exuberant soul who cherished and loved life. A woman fashioned and formed by her years of love and toil, the depth of which I could only imagine.

"I have never experienced a morning sunrise like this one," I said. Daisy remarked that mornings like this were common in this country.

She fixed for me, on this morning, a simple breakfast. I sat down and enjoyed bacon, eggs, potatoes, toast and jam. Daisy herself ate very little that morning. In our conversation she mentioned she had not been feeling well for some time.

I would leave on this morning having arrived only the afternoon before. The hours I spent with Daisy were short and

precious and in Daisy's life of more than eighty years I wonder at the brevity of our time together and the significance
of such a brief encounter. It was as though the magnificence
of the Nebraska sunrise was but a reflection of the heart and
soul of Daisy.

Daisy saw me off about mid-morning. My next stop was
the home of Daisy's son Harley R. Hanson (Dick) and wife
Ollie. They were living on a farm north of Oconto, Nebraska.
It was a beautiful day for riding country roads.

I arrived at Dick and Ollie's mid-afternoon as I remember. What gracious people and wonderful hosts they were.
I visited awhile. Dick had a few things to do that afternoon
and so I would have some time on my own.

I went outside and brought my backpack, duffle and
sleeping bag into the guest room that Ollie had prepared for
my overnight stay. Wow, I guess I would not need my sleeping bag. The room was beautiful, satin sheets, pillowcases and
mints. The furnishings, curtains and guest bath were lovely.
I remember thinking, 'for me?' Had they been expecting a
prince? My belongings looked out of place lying on the floor.

There is something special about people who work and
care for the land. Farmers are genuine and I have found them
to be most always hard-working, caring and honest people.
To survive on the farm those traits are almost a requirement.
Dick and Ollie were busy but they both took the time to welcome me and made me feel comfortable and at home. I truly
felt at home in Nebraska, this state I had heard so many say
was nothing more than a boring ride on the interstate to other more interesting places. They were wrong, they probably
never stopped to explore and get to know its people.

In our initial conversations, Ollie and Dick mentioned
some chalk caves I might be interested in but a few miles
down the road. I had rode by the caves earlier on the way
and had no idea they were even there.

With my camera strapped to the backrest carrier I was off
to explore caves. Bending down a bit I entered into a cave.
What unusual caves these were. These were caves carved

by men. 'What an interesting home these would make.' I thought. As my eyes adjusted to the darkness the cave began to brighten. Everything was white and though the light was limited I could see for quite a distance. I walked ahead as far as I felt was comfortable.

I turned around and looking back at the entrance the scene surprised me. The glow of the afternoon light so bright transformed the grass beyond the entrance into brilliant shades of exquisite green, as I had not seen before, quite remarkable. I went down on my knees and snapped a couple of pictures from this wonderful spot.

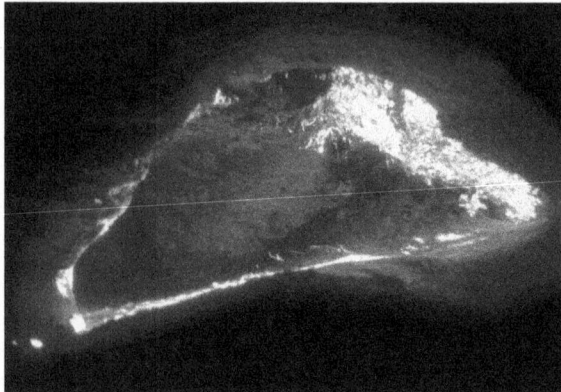

I touched the earth of the cave's floor and the wall. It was indeed chalk. I had used chalk since I was a kid. In all the years, I never thought about where it came from. I stood up, walked back to the cave entrance, and snapped a couple of more pictures. I bent down and walked out of the cave. The land around the caves was gentle and rolling covered in what I supposed were native grasses. There was a quiet about the place, pastoral and peaceful and I sat for a while, relaxing and enjoyed the beautiful late afternoon of a Nebraska day.

I wondered in all the miles of travel on this trip how many treasures had I passed and never knew of anything there. If not for Dick and Ollie, I would have never experienced little treasures that I now enjoyed.

I went back to the farm. In the yard, I noticed berries on a tree, black, like very large blackberries. Dick informed me that it was a Mulberry tree and said they were good to eat. I picked one and it was delicious so I picked a few more of the sweet fruit of the Mulberry tree. That evening we had a very nice supper and it was such a treat to sit in a comfy chair and just relax. I read a few articles in the magazines lying on the lamp stand beside me. The evening was most enjoyable. I slept wonderfully well in the bed of the guest room, and enjoyed the satin sheets and the warmth of the comforter.

Saturday, July 15th

I awoke to a beautiful Nebraska morning. Not the surprise morning I had experienced at Daisy's a little more than twenty-four hours before. Dick and Ollie were up and sitting at the kitchen table. I joined them for breakfast and some good conversation. I then went outside to do some exploring of the farm, buildings, sheds and the like. I picked a handful of treats from the Mulberry tree. As I popped them in my mouth one by one enjoying the sweetness of each berry I was thinking, 'Wish we had one of these trees at my parent's place in Wisconsin.' (*A Mulberry tree now grows on the farm that once belonged to my parents. My brother John and my sister-in-law Sandy now own and live there.*)

I had been on the road for nearly three weeks and was ready for the final leg of the journey home. I went into the house, carried my belongings out to the bike, and strapped everything in its place. "Hello" seems the envious word, "Good-bye" not so much. The good-bye was as good as it gets on this Nebraska blue-sky day. As I left the drive I took one last glance, waved to Dick and Ollie and was on my way. I planned one more stop, Norfolk, a city that was on the route I chose to take me home.

Judy is the daughter of Dick and Ollie and I had not seen her since we were teenagers. In conversation with Dick and Ollie I thought it would be nice to see Judy especially since I would ride so near her place on the route home.

I arrived before noon at the home of Judy *(a granddaughter to Daisy)* who was married and had a little son at the time. Her husband, who I never met, worked as a lawyer if I recall correctly. Judy and I had a very pleasant visit for a couple of hours. She loved Nebraska; its cities were active yet had a small town feel she said. I told her I was enjoying my work in the art field but that it was challenging and competitive in the Minneapolis and St. Paul metro area.

She mentioned that I should give Nebraska some thought as businesses around Norfolk could use my talents. 'Perhaps I would enjoy living here,' I thought. Judy seemed very content in her world and the community in which she lived. Her little boy was such a good little guy. We enjoyed a nice lunch at a little eating-place near her home. Afterwards we visited for a very short time back at her home. It was nice to see Judy once again and her young son.

We said our good-byes and I headed north to Sioux Falls, South Dakota. From there I angled my way east-northeast along country roads, through the many rural towns of southwestern Minnesota along the way. After a leisurely ride the road, I came to the junction with I-35 and I took the busy Interstate the remainder of the way home to St. Paul. Minnesota. Along the way, I pulled over, parked the bike under an overpass, and waited out a sudden downpour of a summer rain. Climbing the incline a ways up from the roadway, I sat waiting out the storm under the bridge.

After waiting out the rain, twenty minutes or so I continued on my way to Saint Paul and arrived in the late afternoon at the home of my sisters. I unpacked most of my belongings and from there headed to Wisconsin and the farm of my parents. After traveling such long distances over the past several weeks, the trip of about sixty miles somehow did not seem so far.

What a wonderful feeling to be home, after three weeks on the road; to ride up the driveway to the farmhouse. I parked the bike and walked up to the front porch door. There to greet me were my youngest sister Grace and Mom. Grace said, "You look like an Indian." A look in the mirror confirmed she was right. I hugged my sister and my mom and as I remember dad was sitting in his chair in the living room. He joined us in the kitchen and we sat for a long visit at the table, in the kitchen of the farmhouse on the hill.

Sunday, July 16th

Sunday was a day of prayer, relaxation, visits with family, friends and much conversation, I am certain. I do not remember the particulars of the day. I only know that the ride west was for me a "trip of a lifetime."

Monday, July 17th

Monday was a workday. A five dollar bill was all that was left in my wallet so it was most reassuring to be back to work again.

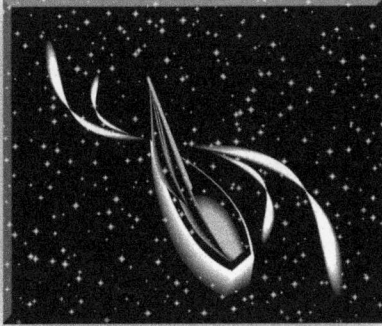

Galaxy 7 *Without A Doubt*

There is freedom on the waters much like the skies above. There are no roadways to follow, though in flying as in boating there are rules of navigation for the safety of pilot and skipper alike and most assuredly any passengers aboard. A sailplane depends upon updrafts of air, a sailboat on the wind.

There is a rhythm to sailing and moments of peace and perfect harmony between wind and sail. And there are those moments of uncertainty, discord and chaos when things suddenly go awry. Times when sheets jamb, lines tangle and rudders break and always when the winds are at their strongest. And so sailors do their best, and nature takes care of the rest.

Lessons are learned and knowledge gained in the experience of sailing and life. And looking back without a doubt, humor and adventure sail through it all.

THERE'S HUMOR SOMEWHERE

Late in the afternoon of a summer day Rick and I pushed a 16' Hobie Cat from a sandy beach into the cool waters of Lake Superior and the Apostle Islands National Lakeshore. Provisions for several days were strapped to the fore of the trampoline. We wore wet-suits and life jackets. Empty milk bottles were duck taped and tied in place, adorning the top of the mast and would serve as floatation in case of the boats capsize. We were ready. For anyone watching it must have been a humorous sight.

A gentle breeze filled the sails as we began the sail to our planned camp on Stockton Island. Somewhere between Madeline Island to the south and Hermit Island to the north we were becalmed in the dusk of the evening. Lights of the city of Bayfield to the southwest disappeared as a night fog quickly formed. A thick surface fog blanketed the waters and in the darkness there was zero visibility. Now what do we do?

Looking up to my surprise, I could see the bright and nearly full moon through the fog. What a comfort to be able to see the soft glow of moonlight piercing through the mist from above. The experience of the sudden loss of visibility had been for me an uncomfortable one. Rick with a paddle in hand asked, "So, what do you think; which island do we head for?" "We're closer to Madeline and it would be hard to miss." I answered. We followed the compass heading in a southern direction while referencing the moon above. At this point in time I was glad my young son David had decided not to go with us on this trip.

So much of what we do is automatic. I recalled just minutes before the fog formed taking in our surroundings and knowing Madeline was the closer island to our position. I figured our location was a half mile or so from its northern shore. We kept taking turns, one of us at the helm and the other at the paddle as we made our way through the fog.

After taking turns at the paddle and helm numerous times we began to hear the waters lapping the shore; but could see nothing before us. Then off to the left we saw a dim fuzz ball of light through the fog, and turning the boat to the east headed for it. As we got closer we could make out the dark line of a dock over the water. We came alongside and tying up stepped onto the deck. It was of metal construction, a dock we figured to be about 75' in length by 8' in width. We walked toward the island rising steeply into the darkness before us. There was a stairway built on the face of the rock of the island; however at this time of night, why climb. Not knowing what was above and needing a place to sleep we decided to make the dock our home for the night. Curious about whose dock this was I wondered what kind of place was above us. For now though I gave thanks for the gift of a dock on which to sleep.

We assembled the tent on the deck and secured it with lines to the below deck, side frames of the dock. We unleashed our sleeping bags and the provisions we needed from the trampoline of the Cat. We hydrated, had a couple of snacks, visited a while and turned in for the night.

I awoke in the very early light of day and in the comfort of the sleeping bag lay for a while just listening. I could hear the sounds of the boat's rigging and the rhythmic bumping of the boat fenders on the side of the dock. The waves were crashing on the rocks of the shore, pushed by winds from the northwest. The fabric of the tent rippled. Rick, having awoken earlier, had adjusted the mooring lines and anchor as the winds grew stronger in the early hours of the morning. He knew as I did that it would be a tricky launch from the dock on this morning as we would be launching into the building waves and strengthening wind.

We each opened a personal sized box of cereal and poured sweetened condensed milk on our cereal, as it was all we had. Yuck; however I managed to down it all. Orange juice and an energy bar or two completed our breakfast.

Removing our gear from the tent onto the deck we dismantled the tent. I stepped onto the trampoline and with the bow rising and falling with each successive wave began to secure the gear. It was not an easy task however. The boat pitched fore and then aft and was in constant motion. Rick remarked how well I was doing considering the movement of the boat.

I was beginning to think that perhaps we would have been better off to have been in the lee of Hermit Island to our north, but no matter; we were where we were.

At last with everything secured we were set to go. Rick did a review of our launch procedure. Due to the shoreline forming a kind of bay where the dock was located there would be little room for error. I pulled anchor and crawled back onto the dock. With the reefed main and jib sail at ease; the Dacron fabric snapped and flapped violently in the wind. Rick and I pushed and pulled the boat up the dock's side and around to the end bringing the hull parallel to its edge.

We positioned the boat fenders between the hull and the end edge of the dock and climbed aboard. Releasing the lines from the dock we quickly eased the main sheet and the jib in and with sails filling the boat gained steerage. We were off and the Hobie shot forward in the strong winds. Lucky for us and the boat it was a perfect launch, all went well and we missed the shore and its rocks with room to spare.

For the first time in my life I took a ride on a flying trapeze. Secure in the trapeze and with feet in the hull straps I stretched out over the water enjoying the ride and the spray. What an exhilarating ride. We sailed for a while in what I am sure were 20 knot plus winds; moving through the waters faster than I had ever sailed before. Rick sailed the Hobie with some caution knowing this was Lake Superior. To pitchpole in these waters could easily prove disastrous.

Sailing a catamaran in a good wind is exciting and fun. I trusted Rick's skills as a sailor and enjoyed the morning's sail immensely.

In our visit to the Park's headquarters we read the warnings about Lake Superior on one of the signs taking note of the line "...boats under 18' are not recommended..." As the Park brochure noted in conclusion, "The Lake is the boss..."

We decided it prudent, given the extremes of the wind and water to call it a day. We made our way over and through the waves and soon we were back at the beach we had launched from only the late afternoon of the day before. Packing up, we set off for home.

Much like Steve Martin, Rick is a kind of wild and crazy guy; (as if the milk jugs, duck taped to the top of the mast in the event of the boats capsize didn't tip you off.) The provisions and gear we strapped to the trampoline were enough for nearly any calamity that might come our way. With paddle, light, batteries, safety flares and compass, I was assured I would be safe and secure with Rick. When we found ourselves becalmed and in the fog, of course I was with Rick. And coming up on a random dock with a light on the north side of Madeline Island; you might say it was providential and I knew it was all because of Rick. And when sweetened, condensed milk was all we had for our cereal, well I think you get the idea; there was a lot of humor mixed with a little adventure on a midsummer's sail.

If you get the chance to visit the Apostle Islands someday, and the wind on the waters fall still; listen carefully in the evening dusk and you might hear laughter echoing from island to island, from something that happened years ago.

Or it could be the call of one of the coyotes that inhabit the islands. You decide.

http://www.nps.gov/apis/index.htm

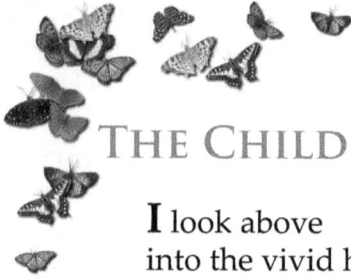

THE CHILD WITHIN

I look above
into the vivid hue
gazing upon love
white clouds on blue

Waiting for birth
in the cool of night
seeds of the earth
longing for light

From earth and the clay
in sacred darkness forms
life and the coming of day
love, the gift of light adorns

Love in my arms
now enters my heart

-rb April 2012

Thoughts on the poem: The Child Within

It was an extraordinary spring day; blue skies and cotton clouds. I was on my knees digging in the earth. I took a break and looked up gazing upon the beauty of sky – it was a first stanza and the beginning.

LET THE FEATHERS FLY

"Really!" I hear,
"That was not very nice."
One more pillow is hurled my way.

I duck, but too late,
"Sorry my dear,
that was a dumb thing to say."

The room fills with laughter,
at what was just said, absent the brain.

What if the bullet was more like the pillow?

-rb

Thoughts on the poem: Let The Feathers Fly

While I helped my wife make the bed one afternoon I can only conjecture that I must have said something not very nice. I have no recollection of what I said but suddenly a pillow came my way. And as I recall the pillow was returned and returned once more as more postage was probably due. That was it, but for the amen of the laughter.

There is a line from the Disney film Bambi, when Thumper, after saying something not very nice was reminded by his mother of what his father had told him. Thumper recalled and haltingly spoke, "If you can't say something nice, don't say nothin' at all."

A ONE AND A...

Oh, how I love to sing,
how I enjoy a good song.

When life is heavy
it lightens the load.

Today I join with others
to sing,
to pray
to love.

-rb

*A poem, based on writing I found in the cabinet containing
the archives of my work – a few simple lines dated March 2, 2001*

THE GIFT

A darkened sky
stars but a memory
of what was...
but is that not
what a star should be

I longed...
for what once was
the sky of my youth
when in darkness
there was light

I now know
that even in darkness
peace is found
for the light
seen or unseen
is always there

Lay me down
on a blanket of ground
soft upon the earth
trust in the goodness of another

The sky in darkness
how bright the stars shine
the stars I longed to see
the stars I knew
all along
were shining on me

Trust in the goodness of another
and love is found
in the gift of light
the wonder of sight
and the peace of the night

It is Christmas
and I think of you
and the goodness I have found.

-rb A reflection on a Christmas night, 2011

Thoughts on the poem: The Gift

Following eye surgery it is difficult to put into words my gratitude for the gift of restored vision, a vision I have not experienced, but perhaps only as a young boy. I remember looking with wonder at the night stars in those the days of my youth. On a late evening, early in October 1957 my father and I searched among the stars appearing in the darkening skies, for the sunlight reflecting off the satellite Sputnik. I am not certain whether or not we succeeded in our search but I treasure that moment in time shared with my father.

SARDINES

I've much empathy
for the little sardine
packed in the can
with the shining gleam.

What does they do
for recreation
no longer able
to swim about creation.

-rb

*Penned while waiting out a summer rain storm
in a 1981 Pontiac T1000 – a rather small compact car*

Thoughts on the poem: Sardines

It had been a nice afternoon. I was dating my wife-to-be Barb at the time and we decided it might be nice to spend an hour or so canoeing on Lake Harriet and then relax at Fireside Pizza afterwards. I drove to her family home in South Minneapolis. We took her car, a compact, blue in color, 3 door hatchback, stick-shift, Pontiac T1000, for the drive to the lake. She drove and as we approached the drive around the lake it began to rain. We parked in a lot just as it began to pour.

We listened to the radio and visited awhile and the heavy rain continued. We both decided in a moment of complete agreement that we would not be canoeing on this day. So, now what do we do? "I'll write you a poem" I said. And so I took a pen from the glove box, found a piece of paper and a book for backing and began to write.

I kept the poem and its lines to myself as I wrote. As the poem developed I began to think, 'What might Barb be expecting; something romantic? If so she'll be disappointed. Maybe she isn't expecting much of anything as I had never done a poem before, at least not for her, "Sardines" was penned in about 15 minutes from beginning to end.

"Well," I said, "here you go." She read it and we both laughed. She handed it back to me and remarked, "Funny and creative." It was a perfectly appropriate poem for our situation on that late afternoon as we sat in a compact car and pouring rain. The rain let up some and so we left the lot on Harriet and drove to Fireside Pizza and had a lovely time.

I kept the poem and sometime later decided to frame it and give it to Barb as a gift. How do I frame a poem, special for the one I love? 'Ah, the sardine can. Barb will love it. Not!' I enjoy sardines once in a while, Barb does not. I first looked in the recycle box but there was no sardine can and so I looked in my cupboard and found two cans of sardines, one with a key and one without. I took the can with the key as that might add some interest to the framing for the poem. I opened the can, sat down and enjoyed the sardines with some cheese and crackers. I then washed and rinsed the can, dried it well and placed the poem within. I found a clear plastic shadow box frame just the right size and placed the tin within.

Barb loved the gift I gave her.

I keep the framed poem in my office. Sometimes when things don't go as planned, the poem reminds me, don't worry, be happy, flexible and know that with some thought and a bit of creativity, all will be right.

Galaxy 8 *Left Overs; Gotta Love'em*

Ooglee, the name of a little oobling, came about because sometimes I hear what I want to hear and not what I do hear. And the same goes for the seeing. It's a brain thing. Typos in this book are a perfect example. *(And there must be a few.)*

Sometime in the summer of 1981 a little creature appeared on my drawing board. It was a quick, simple drawing of a figure. One afternoon while visiting with friends; I presented the little character for comment. Debbie took a look and astonishingly quick declared, "Oh, a little oobling." I did not quite hear what she had said. Nothing is ever simple for me and so I tried to make sense of what I thought I just heard, "Ooglee?" I asked. "No," Oobling, she said. "Oobling," I repeated. "Hmm, I misunderstood you; so what do you think of Ooglee?" I asked. In further conversation the name Ooglee was approved and Oobling came to refer to the name for the species of the new found life form.

Galaxy 8 is from Ooglee's scrapbook of life. With the following Ooglee comment, "Billowing clouds and billowing sails make for a delicate balance," I now present the well balanced excerpts of thought and gentle laughs from the life of Ooglee. And so, without further ado, "Here's Ooglee."*(Ooglee now awaits your turning of the page.)*

OOGLEE - THE LITTLE OOBLING

One day I walked into the office of Ernie,
for Ernie is a friend of mine.
"What have you there?" he asked.
I lifted the cover of my drawing board.
"Oh, just a friend who suddenly appeared,
to my surprise," was all I said.
"What is its name?" Ernie asked.
"Ooglee," I said.
"Where is the creature from?" he inquired.
Well, I really could not surmise.
"Somewhere I guess...
So, tell me Ernie, perhaps you know."
And we sat and talked a while as we so often did,
"See you in a day or two," I said, and off I went.

One day I walked into the office of Ernie,
for Ernie is a friend of mine.
He held up an envelope, handed it to me.
I began to read and to my surprise,
was a story of Ooglee I never knew.

On the eight following pages is the story written by my
dear friend Ernie. *If only everyone had a friend like Ernie.*
    The sketches accompanying the text are of a storyboard
I worked up soon after reading the story for the first time.
Drawing is one of the many things I love to do. Enjoy!

A STORY OF THE LITTLE OOBLING, OOGLEE

...from the very beginning as the author imagined it to be...
written by Ernie Forss
Story board illustrations - character and the name Ooglee...
by Bob Buckner

On the very last day of Creation, when God was finished up in the heavenly workshop, God had some stuff left over.

Because he was in a hurry to quit for the week, God shoved all the left over stuff together into a capsule.

Stuff that angels are made of and stuff that people are made of were all stored up together. And then God rested.

God got so busy after the day of rest, with apples, floods, pillars of salt and all, that the capsule was left to sit for years and years.

Many years later the angel who is called the Spirit of Little Children (SLC) was playing in the workshop and found the capsule.

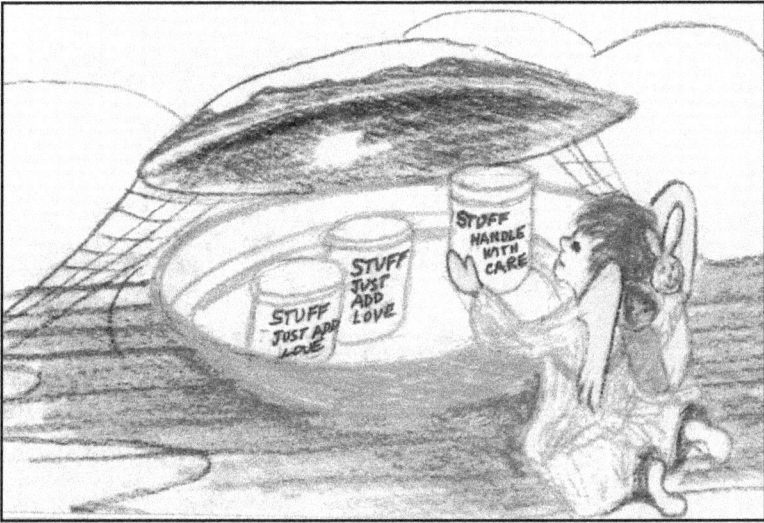

It was like a spaceship or so SLC thought but it was all sealed up. The Spirit of Little Children broke open the capsule and found all the left over stuff of Creation.

The angel decided to surprise God by building a person. Because there was only some stuff left over from Creation the Spirit of Little Children had to make do and fashion a little character as best he could.

Also in the capsule of left over stuff were supplies of natural goodness which the angel poured in.

And there was a fair amount of desire left over: desire to do good, desire to be happy, desire to help, and desire to love.

All these things went into the new creation. And then at the bottom left over from Creation, the Spirit of Little Children found oodles and oodles of gentle laughs and endless energy.

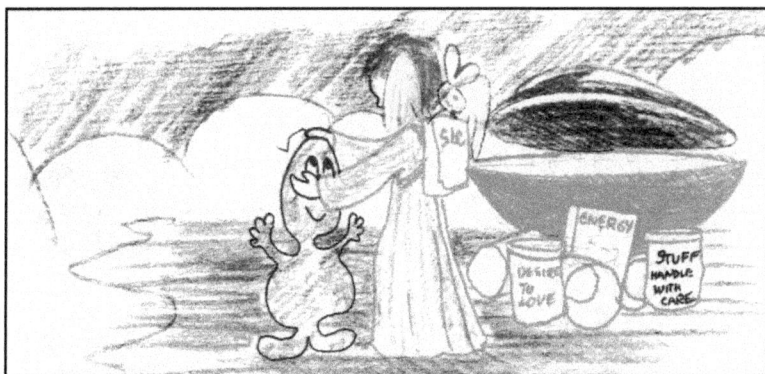

Because the Spirit of Little Children just loves all of these things, the whole supply of the oodles were poured in and the new little creation took shape.

The Spirit of Little Children brought all of this in to show God who had to laugh when He saw it because it was such a mixture of Creation.

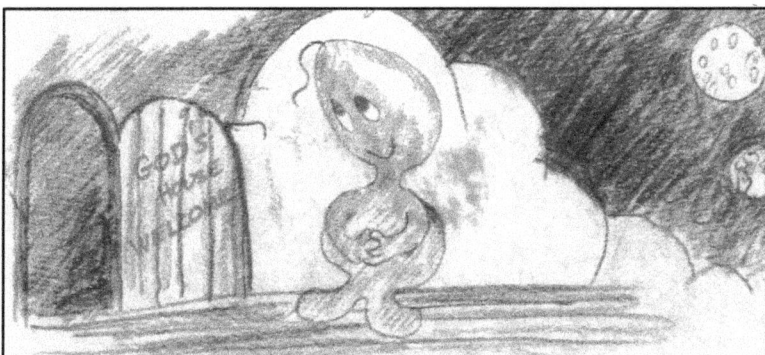

It was not quite an angel, and not quite a human but a lot of each.

And God was so delighted that He breathed life into it and God told the Spirit of Little Children to name this new little creation.

SLC said, "The name is Oodles and Oodles of Gentle Laughs and Endless Energy, because that is what I mostly put into it." God laughed while the Spirit giggled.

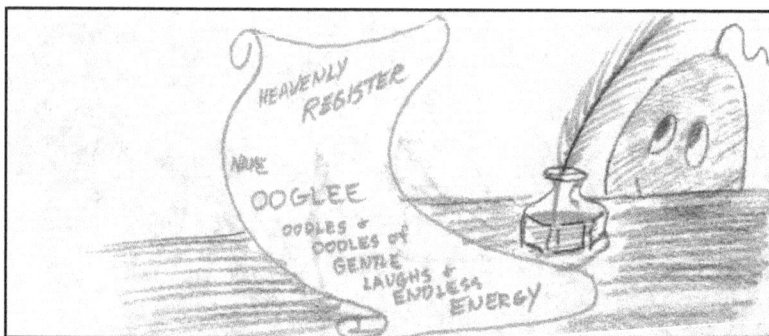

But God said, "That is too long a name. We will abbreviate it. The name is Ooglee which will stand for Oodles and Oodles of Gentle Laughs and Endless Energy."

Now, being made of some stuff of Angels Ooglee should be able to go anywhere, but since some of the stuff was of people Ooglee wasn't able to do so.

And so God made the capsule, in which SLC had found the left over stuff of Creation, into a spaceship and brought it to Ooglee who was delighted.

It was just the right size for Ooglee and had just enough power to go anywhere in the universe.

But it is only people who know the Spirit of Little Children that can know Ooglee, because only in that spirit can we know oodles and oodles of gentle laughs and endless energy which are the basis of God's creative love.

THE END

DREAMS

As I have read and re-read Ooglee's story of creation I have often closed my eyes and I thought of Ernie. The story is so "Ernie" and so "Bob" and so all of us!

Like the capsule with all the stuff of Creation left over we all have dreams that we have stored in our own capsules. Every day we work and go about our daily lives and the dreams we have remain just what they are. DREAMS.

I believe dreams resolve and when all is said and done everything will be alright! It's just something I think is possible.

And so I share with you, Ooglee, a little dreamer.

The angel decided to surprise God by building a person. Because there was only some stuff left over from creation, the Spirit of Little Children (SLC) had to make do and fashion a little character as best it could.

I Am Me.

I may not look
so much like you...
I am me
and have a right to be.
Please don't fear me
I am different
as you can see
but it's what you don't see
that makes you
very much like me!

A poem by the little oobling, Ooglee

One of my earlier poems is found within an early portrait of Ooglee. (facing page) The poem is titled, "I Am Me."

A background for the poem.

It has been my honor and joy to know and work for persons with developmental disabilities since I was a young man in my teens. I remember thinking, "How different they are from me." Through the years I gradually became aware of who they, we, all are. We are so very much the same.

Years ago I volunteered as a staff person on a retreat for developmentally disabled adults at Villa Maria Retreat Center in Frontenac, Minnesota sponsored at the time by the College of St. Thomas. It was on one of these retreats that I penned the poem, **I Am Me**. It was "a life changing moment." The poem I attribute to Ooglee, who is so very much like me and all of us really.

O*oglee's vital and not so vital information**:

Age: Forever young
Sex: Hmm
Height: Flexible
Weight: Depends
Hair: What's it matter? Ok, one, curly
Skin: Colorful
Eyes: Two – sparkling
Mouth: One – smiles
Tummy: Not fussy
Donor: Yes! A good heart to be shared with everyone.

*As noted on Ooglee's saucer license.

MINNESOTA
SHAPED BY LOTS OF HUGS

Minnesota! There is so much to see and do in Minnesota. Lakes, rivers, streams abound throughout the state. Parks in abundance welcome visitors to the natural beauty of woodlands, lakes, streams and waterfalls, grasslands and prairie, marshlands, fields and forests. No wonder Minnesota is so loved by so many.

STATE OF MINNESOTA
Office of the Governor
ST. PAUL 55155

RUDY PERPICH
GOVERNOR

April 18, 1989

Robert Buckner
P.O. Box 2086
Stillwater, Minnesota 55082

Dear Robert:

I would like to take this opportunity to thank you for the
Minnesota "Ooglee" picture that you left at my office recently.

Your gift, and others I have received, remind me of your
generosity and that of the many people I meet in my capacity as
Governor of Minnesota. Your gift will become part of the
historical record of my tenure as Governor, one that will be
shared by the people of Minnesota in the future.

Once again, thank you for your generosity.

Sincerely,

RUDY PERPICH
Governor

AN EQUAL OPPORTUNITY EMPLOYER

OOGLEE VISITS THE GOVERNOR

When Ooglee discovered the shape that Minnesota was
in he decided to have a visit with Rudy Perpich, Minnesota's
governor at the time. By the date of the letter it looks like the
letter was written a while ago and the shape of Minnesota
after all those years is still the same. Judging from the rather
nice letter Ooglee must have had a cordial meeting.

OOGLEE, PRAGUE AND THE CZECH REPUBLIC

What a wonderful city, country and people. Prague seems more like a fairyland, though Prague is very "Real," rich in its people and history. As Ooglee strolled along a street not far from the Old Castle Steps the little Oobling came across this graffiti on a wall. Ooglee stopped and took this picture in the fall of 1995. No signature of the artist was to be found for I would imagine graffiti is frowned upon, perhaps most especially in Prague. Somehow, this wall had quite a lot of graffiti on it as you can see the lines of other works. This particular drawing done by whoever, stood out and is a fine work of art.

If you get the chance to visit Prague, Ooglee says, "Just do it." Ooglee would be happy to take you on the tour and might even hold the umbrella just so you don't get lost. Now there is a good little Oobling.

AN OOGLEE ALBUM OF LIFE

The images on the next few pages are some of my favorite drawings, snapshots if you will, in the life of Ooglee, a little wanderer amidst the stars, stuck for a time, but rather pleased to be here with us on this special planet teaming with life and wonder called Earth. For now it is Ooglee's home.

I call it the **SMILE** phase!

I wonder what happens if an umbrella sees its shadow?

All day and noth'n' – Do you suppose the fish don't like my bait?

Why... I think you're a **GREAT** Valentine!

A roller coaster like life, wouldn't be much fun if not for the ups and downs.

PIZZA... The cheese is rather like a Wrestling Buddy.

A word about Ooglee's saucer - The little saucer from time to time heads for the starry heavens from which it came. But then returns. And so the little Oobling is still around, living a life full of happiness on this Earth; Ooglee's other spaceship. Ooglee has found a home here, and there is not another place quite like it in all the universe. Meanwhile Ooglee continues to live up to the name spreading Oodles & Oodles of Gentle Laughs and Endless Energy right here on this earthly planet with you.

Billowing clouds and billowing sails make for a delicate balance.

Ah... The life of a frog; until the BIG FISH comes along.

And so the idea of fast food began...

Corn is aMAIZEing! Just think, the classic fairy tale entitled Jack & the Cornstalk.

Maybe I look like another rock in the pond, or just maybe it thinks I'm its mom or dad.

Yours is a fanciful flight on delicate wings little butterfly.

LOOKS LIKE NO ONE CAUGHT YOU LITTLE STAR!

There is a song composed by Lee Pockriss and Paul Vance, and recorded in 1957 by Perry Como titled, "Catch a Falling Star." It is one of those tunes that nearly sings itself. I have always enjoyed the song, both lyrically and as well, the simplicity of its melody. Judging by the caption above Ooglee must enjoy it too.

OOGLEE'S WORLD

I dreamed I was a butterfly,
I awoke and there I was.

People are like popcorn,
when the heat's on they react.

Amazing! No instruments,
no flaming tails.

Did you ever try to bite into gold?
When I'm hungry you are worth
so very much more.

OOGLEE'S WORLD

Distance apart 5"x 5"x 5"x 5"x 5"...
and they looked so close together.
As Einstein might say "It's relative."

Sometimes we forget little tree,
how important you really are.

We're both mostly water
but how very different we are.

The cows must keep busy
month after month...
supplying milk for the cheese.

SUNRISE

I fell quite asleep
in this little farm shed.
Morning came,
I sat up from my bed.
There before me,
in front of my eyes
a tapestry of silk,
an intricate surprise.
Wondrously woven
covered with dew.
Nice job Spider!
Was it really you?

COULD YOU

Could you ever imagine
a class of boats
such as the one
that Ooglee floats?

Elegantly simple
jerry rigged by design
sailed by Ooglee
makes very good time.

With plunger on saucer
how fun would that be
a sailing event
I would love to see.

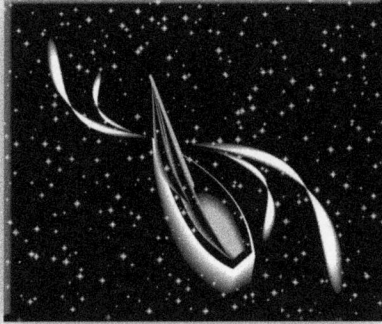

Galaxy 9 *Simpler Times*

Fruit and produce came packed in small wooden crates when I was young. The first boats I built as a kid were made from the wood of such crates. Removing the thin side boards from the thicker end boards, rectangular in shape, I would saw two of the corners diagonally to a point on one end and drill a hole for the mast. Lashing a yardarm to the mast with a string I would then tie a square of fabric to the yardarm. Then it was off I go to a large puddle, tub or small pond for hours of fun.

The line drawings of Galaxy 9 were inked for nothing more than the joy of drawing. Drawn from my memories and based on time spent in the farmlands of my youth, many of these scenes would be difficult to observe in the rural landscapes of today. As I viewed the drawings I wondered, 'would these scenes have much relevance to viewers much younger than myself?'

It is said, "A picture is worth a thousand words." Certainly it is true if the subject is understood. At the same time there is much about a picture that remains unknown; thoughts, lost in the shadows of time, stories known only to the artist. And so I have written brief stories for each of the drawings; reflections of selected moments in time.

And now I bid you welcome to simpler times.

Hay Wagon

High atop the wagon load of hay I sat, when suddenly a timber dropped from the cradle of the wagon frame. Tipping precariously, I looked over the high side for but a moment. Too high, and in another moment down the cascading bales I slid onto the grass of the field below. That was fun, can we do it again? The rest of the story was work.

The Garden

Tilling the soil with a fork was a back-aching, blister forming sort of job. It is not to be rushed for it is a job measured not by minutes but by hours, perhaps even days given the size of the plot.

It always helped to meditate on the growing season ahead. To plant seeds into the earth is an act of faith. After a few days the first of the seeds sprout forth, breaking the soil, leaves unfurling and forming. Days go by and plants mature, blossoms appear. More days pass while the fruit of the plants form.

I think of all that follows, the harvests to come. Carefully I snap a pod from the plant, break open the delicate shell and strip peas into my open hand, "goodness, how delicious."

And before I know it, a day's work is done. Next year, it's the neighbor's tractor.

Prairie Ships

One fall, between jobs as an artist, I exchanged a brush for a hammer and canvas for boards.

The framework of a new barn rests, waiting for the sheathing to be nailed to the frames enclosing the mow. The old barn visible from this vantage point would soon disappear. I wondered how long the old barn would remain.

As I looked at the roof rafters above, hand fastened and assembled, my arms aching, I thought of the immigrant, the builders of barns from centuries before. Many of them built ships for the oceans and brought their knowledge and skill to a new and different ocean of prairie. The barns they built were in very many ways like the ships on an ocean.

Frost Fantasy

One evening, the milking nearly done, I climbed the boards of the hay chute, going from the warm moist air below into the cold December air above, nearly to the peak of the barn. The bare, incandescent bulb hanging from the rafters illuminated a fantasy land of frost all about me. Frost, like stalactites of a cavern, hung from the ropes and the rafters above and like a blanket, frost covered the bales of hay below.

My feet firm on the top board of the chute, I leaned my back against the hay and looking out through the cracks of the barn boards observed the stars. I wondered at the gift of life that was mine and the beauty of this cold December night.

At the time this scene was inked there were no personal computers, cell phones and wireless devices connecting us wherever we went. The utility pole and mailbox were the connection. Letters written by hand and stuffed in a paper envelope or conversations on phone lines shared by neighbor and stranger alike were the norm. I wonder sometimes, if our connectivity today has changed us for the better. In today's instant messaging, are thoughtfulness, patience and perhaps some other virtues now forgotten?

White Pine

On my grandparents last farm, the farm my parents lived in during my dad's retirement years, there is a grove of stately white pine. The southernmost pine of the bunch stands somewhat removed from the rest. This pine was hit at least a couple of times by lightning and all that remains today is a silhouette of the lower portion of the tree and a few bare branches. My father transplanted a dozen seedlings, some from the road ditch to enhance the grove; "his twelve apostles" he called them. Most still stand.

Wisconsin Stable

This was the kind of Christmas creche my dad built for us. It is reminiscent of the simple sheds and small barns, a style ubiquitous to the rural places of the Midwest and from what I have seen, in other places of the world as well. I call it the "Wisconsin Stable."

Visiting the creche I would feel sorry for Mary, Joseph and the baby Jesus as I shivered in the cold until I realized it was not quite so cold in Bethlehem, the place of Jesus' birth.

Tree House

Many trips with the old iron wheeled wheelbarrow were made by us kids hauling lumber, windows, hardware, nails and whatever salvaged or discarded materials we found. Nails, pulled from old boards were used a second time, straightened and pounded into weathered old boards hardened by the years.

The old maple tree sat on the edge of the woods bordering a field. Many carefree summer days as well as a few nights were spent in the cradle of its branches.

Woodpile

The woodpile under this tree was a reserve set aside for the winter if the main piles of wood were not enough. The barn in the distance was the farm of a long time neighbor to my grandparents. I worked for the farmer one summer and at the end of our summer stay, he asked me what he owed me. I declared $25.00 and he wrote out a check. I received a hot lunch every day I worked and would have gladly worked for nothing. I think he felt better that I received something. My mom thought the amount too generous.

Wagon Wheel

Sometimes one wheel on a wagon works just fine as long as it is not rolling. As youngsters one of our favorite pastimes was flying kites. We flew kites literally for hours. When called for lunch the line was tied to whatever was available. We'd be quick with our lunch and it was out the door again. We'd look for the kite and more often than not it was still aloft, carried by the breeze.

I recall introducing Andy, our youngest boy, to the art of kite flying. We walked to an open area in our neighborhood. There seemed some reluctance at first as I instructed Andy on the fine art of kite flying. Thinking back I do remember a bit of intimidation as a child myself as I imagined myself in the air with the kite. A fear of heights perhaps? It wasn't long, much to my chagrin, before Andy and his kite were best of friends.

Oh, and then there was the tree! The bane of kite flying kids and a parent as well. The life span of a kite is not very long.

Summer Days

The summers we spent on "the old Klingelhut place," were some of the best days of my youth. It was the third farm on which my grandparents lived and worked. It was a place of family gatherings, of grandpa, grandma, uncles, aunts, cousins, neighbors, and friends. It was a place of hiking the woods, fishing the creek, picking wild berries, building tree houses, chasing butterflies, catching fireflies and sleeping under the stars. For a city kid who loved the country it was a summer paradise.

*The farm home of my grandparents –"the old Klingelhut place,"
and the home of my parents during their retirement years.*

*An Allis-Chalmers 1927 model E. four cylinder 20-35 tractor
from the collection of Herman Pieper of Jordan, Minnesota.
The photo was taken in the late 1970's or early 1980's.*

This photo was of a tree house built in the mid 1960's located in a wooded area on my parent's farm where we spent much of our summer as youngsters.

A tree swing in the yard of the farm house.

Galaxy 10 · Mercy & Love

When all seems lost, and all that can be done is done, then, and only then, is the time of surrender. There is a place within where fear and pain cannot go. It is the harbor of mercy and love, the moment of stillness and peace in the midst of the raging storm.

In all the times I have set sail there is only one thing I can be certain of and that is uncertainty. A sail is never the same experience twice for the environment from which it draws its energy is so incredibly random.

The problem I have with love is I keep thinking it is simple when I know it is not. I keep thinking that it comes without hardship, struggle, pain, grief or sorrow. If only love was a calm sea. The problem is, we wouldn't move or grow, we wouldn't reach the distant shores and new worlds that lie ahead.

Galaxy 10 • Mercy & Love is a story of family, of community, hope and love. It is story of the doldrums of addiction, the fair weather of peaceful moments and the raging seas of poverty and pain. And in its ending, a story of mercy and love.

FRANCIS, THE UNCLE I NEVER KNEW
but for the memories of those who loved him

Prologue

I never intended to write the story of Francis. It began as three sheets of paper on which were written a rather simple outline of the story as my mother had shared with me but a few days prior. I wrote so as not to forget the story. I read what I had outlined and could only wonder, who was Francis? What was he like? What was it like to live in his time, the time of my mother, aunt, and uncles? My grandpa and grandma to my recollection had never mentioned their son, Francis. I wondered why? Mom's sharing of her story of Francis, and the story of her youth became for me a labor of love.

I gave the manuscript to my mother a couple of years after finishing the story of Francis. I continued to see Mom as often as I could and the story was never mentioned. It would be several years until she would read the story.

Four of Uncle Ralph's five girls traveled to Pine City, Minnesota one summer day to visit their Aunt Barb. They visited as families do and I can imagine the gentle heartfelt conversations and joy of their time together. Jane, at the time, was working on gathering information on her family ancestry. At some point Mom dug out a few of the things she had collected and saved through the years. Along with her things was the manuscript of the story of "Francis." My cousins began to scan through the pages of the story and asked if they might make copies and so they did. It was a day with her nieces Mom so enjoyed.

Mom had not yet read the story and with the visit of her nieces decided it was time. Within a few days of their visit Mom finally sat down with the manuscript and read the story of Francis. She later told me, "It was strange to read a story from my youth written by a son who was never there." Pausing for a moment she added, "It is a good story..."

The epilogue of the story I wrote after Mom's death. Though Mom never read the epilogue, I believe in her loving and caring heart she already knew the story's ending.

The story is based on my mother's memories and those of my uncles and others who knew Francis, my mother and her parents. It is a story that I retell from my time, place and the experience of my life.

A photo taken at Camp 9 School showing students and teacher Fannie Biddle –
Francis is the middle boy in the bottom row.

As September arrives summer fades and the hints of autumn begin. Leaves transform from the cool shades of summer to the warm shades of autumn. The days are shorter, more intense and the dusk of evening comes quickly. School begins and the ebb and flow of everyday life settles into its familiar fall routine. For me a part of autumn's routine begins with Wednesday evening's church choir practice. Light filters down from lamps where the choir practices. The greater sanctuary area remains in darkness. One evening as voices transformed the cavernous space into music, a cricket chirped as if to join in the celebration. I suddenly remembered my grandpa and grandma and was transported back to another place and time.

When I was a young boy I spent many days and nights with mom, dad and my brothers and sisters on grandpa and grandma's farm. In late summer as the light of day gave way to the night, the chirp of crickets amplified into the darkness. How I enjoyed the warmth, light and love of that farmhouse on a summer's night. The radio crackled as the last polkas played and the station signed off at the end of another day. Grandma played her games of solitaire and Grandpa sat in the rocker, his spittoon alongside. It was truly another place and time.

Just before bedtime we kids made a final trip into the darkness and out to the outhouse. Always we went two or three at a time as it was just too scary to make the trip alone. The smells of the outhouse were at times a bit much and the chamber pot which was used as a night time indoor toilet was always an unpleasant smell and its contents emptied each morning into the outhouse pit. Such was life on the farm in the years before indoor plumbing.

There were as I remember, distinctive, almost pleasant aromas to grandpa and grandma's house. It was probably a combination of many things, the old wood flooring with its varnish, the throw rug carpets and other furnishings. Perhaps too there was the mix of damp air rising though the floor boards from the basement and its foundation which in the springtime especially would often become quite wet.

Often we slept on the carpet of the living room floor or sometimes in one of the bedrooms upstairs. And most wonderfully most days we awoke to the smell of breakfast, buttered biscuits, bacon, fried potatoes and another new day.

As a child I could not know the struggles or sorrows that my parents or grandparents went through. All I knew and cared about was the security of parents and grandparents who loved me.

When not at my grandparent's Wisconsin farm our family lived in Minnesota. I was born in Wisconsin and when I was three years old the family moved to St. Paul Park, Minnesota where we lived until I was nine years of age.

Summers as a youth were spent outdoors chasing butterflies and catching grasshoppers in the fields that surrounded our home. Kite flying was another favorite thing to do. I remember watching the clouds float by in the day and the starry sky of night. One early evening I remember being outside with my dad searching for Sputnik as that first satellite made its way across the sky.

Winters were spent playing indoors or when there was snow, and it wasn't too cold, we spent hours sliding down the hill behind the house.

In the early morning darkness and cold one late winter morning I recall waiting at a bus stop with my mother and father. I was the firstborn and at the time had two younger sisters. I shivered in the cold and my teeth chattered. Dad wrapped his arms around me to warm me as we waited at the stop. The bus arrived and took us to the train station in St. Paul. There we boarded the Zephyr and traveled to Elgin, Illinois. I remember climbing the stairs into the vista dome of one of the train cars. That is about all I remember of the trip to Illinois.

My mom's sister, my Aunt Cele, was very sick. I remember her lying in a hospital bed, a clock on the wall and a discussion about time. I had no conception of dying or of time. A few weeks later she died. My grandparents, mom and my uncles traveled to Illinois for her funeral.

Later as I grew older I remember my mom telling of a brother, my Uncle Francis who died many years before I was born. He was leading one of the work horses and died of his injuries after the horse spooked and then bolted across the pasture dragging Francis as it ran. As a boy I thought of Francis and later because of my uncle's name became very interested in Francis, the Saint of Assisi. Mom would often read to us from a children's book of saints. I loved to hear the story within the book, of St. Francis, a village and a wolf.

When I reached the age for Confirmation in my Catholic/Christian faith, part of the tradition at the time was to take the name of a saint as a confirmation name. I took the name of Francis, partly as a remembrance of my uncle, and partly because I liked the stories told of the Saint, Francis.

Now that I am older and have experienced life's struggles and sorrows in the mix of joy, I've thought about what my mother and grandparents lived through in a time and place far removed from my own. And still the strings of time continue to weave the experiential tapestry of our lives.

The mother of a dear friend died during the winter on one of the earlier days of 2001. She was born in the early part of the 1900s. My mother accompanied me to the funeral held at Moe Lutheran, a small country church in rural western Wisconsin. On the drive home my mother and I conversed about her life as a young girl and of her brother Francis. I said then said to her, "I know I have heard the story before but it has been quite some time ago and there is so much I do not remember."

And so she began...

FRANCIS, THE UNCLE I NEVER KNEW

But for the memories of those who loved him

The Jackelen family from left to right: Francis, Frank, Ben, Barb, Ralph, Lawrence, Mary and Cele. Val, the youngest is not shown in this photo.

Farm Life

The earth gave way and folds of ground lay drying in the noonday sun. As the blade of the plow tore through the sod of the field, roots lamented in a barely perceptible symphony of sound. Fanny and Blackie pulled hard against the harness. Frank, his strong hands on the plow scanned the furrows of newly turned earth. The horses had begun to slow as the sun reached its apex in the sky. 'About an acre and a half of new plowed ground, done since the early morning chores. It was a good start on the plowing of the field,' Frank thought. After this row he would head the horses for water and rest. The last field left to plow this spring would soon be done.

Fanny and Blackie were good strong horses, pulled well together and were well mannered. Frank cared for them as best he could. They were, he knew, the means to life on farms like his amid the wooded, rolling land of western Wisconsin. Without a good team of horses there would be no planting or harvesting of crops that kept the cattle fed.

In many ways Frank was not much of a farmer though. It was what he did however, year after year. So many of the chores were mundane, tedious and every day was the same as the next. The last summer was hot and dry. After all the toil and the harvest, there was not much to show for. It was a frustrating business. Too much rain, not enough, too cold, too hot, that was the life of the farmer. Farming was an occupation of extremes and always there was work and little to show for at the end of a day.

Val, the seventh child, had just been born and Frank wondered how little or nothing could be divided one more time. There was so much that was out of Frank's control. The wood had run out in late winter and in desperation Frank cut trees, the wood still green, to feed the stove. Green wood provided little heat but plenty of smoke. He wondered about the chance of a chimney fire caused by the buildup of sap from the smoke of green wood smoldering in the stove. Ma lamented about the smoke, how it burned her eyes, how long it was taking to boil water for the cooking of food or the washing of clothes that accumulated fast with a family now numbering nine. "If it makes my eyes water what about the kids?" she told Frank. The hay and the corn had run low and because he was forced to ration it, milking the cows was hardly worth the trouble. Even the lard from the last butchered hog was running low and was now rather rancid. Frank, troubled in mind and spirit, longed for solace that would not come but for moments rare indeed.

Indeed, Frank could relate to the Job fellow in the Old Testament. But when he tried to meditate on that story and seek some kind of consolation he found little, for he considered Job a good and upright man in the eyes of God. Not a man filled with shame as he was. Job, good and upright was the piece in the story that didn't seem to fit for Frank. He hated himself for the things he did; the drinking, the resultant temper and the rage which welled up inside. Frank knew he was out of control more often than not. He drank far too much of the alcoholic brew which was so much a part of the social gatherings of family and friends. Frank in silence had said 'no' to the urge for another drink a thousand times and more. He would often add perhaps a day or two of sobriety to his life but the demon in the bottle eventually would have its day.

Church was important to Frank, his mother made sure of that for as long as he could remember. He looked for solace there. He received the sacraments as a young boy and lived life as best he could. At times he even felt the consolation found in the rituals and the sacraments of the church though he barely understood the where or the why of it all. The moments of precious peace he did find when sober were often wanting and now as he was growing older seemed to evade him more and more. When he did pray, he pleaded and begged for some kind of resolution in his life.

Frank was an honored man, well-spoken of by many in the community. Those who knew him well also knew the darker side of his drunkenness. He was as fine a man as any when he was sober and his wife Mary, more than anyone, knew that much about the one she loved. The problem was he was so seldom sober. Mary carried the sorrow of loss deep within her heart. The loss of dreams and the love of a man she once knew vanished long ago in the hopeless drudgery of her daily toil.

Social gatherings were a welcome oasis to the hard toil of farming. It was at one of these gatherings that Frank and Mary first met. Oh how Frank and Mary loved to dance! When they were dancing nothing else seemed to matter. Frank loved the music and was blessed with a natural sense of rhythm and voice, so much a part of his family's Germanic heritage and that of most of his friends. He learned to fiddle early in his youth and played often at the many gatherings and celebrations that were such an important part of the fabric of rural life. Frank and Mary were married during WWI. Frank joined the army but soon after enlisting the war came to an end. When he returned home from the service he and Mary bought their farm and continued their lives together.

The feel of the reins as they came near to the edge of the field told Fanny and Blackie this would be the last row of this morning's workout. The horses, sweaty and covered with the dirt and dust of the field, stood patiently as the plow was unhitched. The morning breeze had been working the windmill and the water tank would be full. Water, feed and rest awaited them. Frank led the horses to the barn pleased with the progress of the day. He would let the horses rest and plow again in the latter part of the day. The three oldest of the seven kids would arrive home from school by mid-afternoon and would do the afternoon and evening chores. Frank would again return to the field and complete the ritual of plowing.

Frank hung the harness on the sideboards of the stall. He glanced at the few feed sacks remaining and calculated whether they might last 'til the pastures greened and the hard fieldwork of spring was done. Frank thought of the bottle stored among the sacks of feed. He longed for a drink. For some days now he had passed it by but today would not be the same as the previous days. The liquor would consume the next several days of his life. It would be days before the plowing of the two acres or so of the last field would be finished. The planting would again be late putting the crops at risk if the summer was hot and dry and the fall freeze came early.

Frank soon found himself uncorking the bottle of brew. He sat on a sack of feed and let his mind drift. The past winter had seemed horribly long and cold. He was grateful the house had not burned to the ground and that spring had at last arrived. The spring had suddenly warmed and filled the land with greening and the promise for another growing season and with it the promise of easier times. It was too hot for this time of year though. Frank doubted this season would be any different than the sun scorching dryness of the previous summer. 'Out of one extreme and into another again,' he thought. Frank knew the effect of the drink would soon put his mind to rest and remove the agony and torment that whirled within.

A farmer toiled from dawn to dusk, year after year 'til sickness, accident or old age put an end to the merciless toil. If one was lucky, a farmer would live to an old age; a son would take over the work and a daughter or daughter-in-law would nurse them in their old age. His own parents were getting older and his sisters, Margaret and Josie, lived with them and would care for them as they entered into their old age. Frank had thought about that often as he cared for the grounds of the church cemetery or dug the graves for a deceased member of the parish.

Digging graves was one of the few rituals that seemed to bring a kind of solace to his being. It was the final act of love he could do for a fellow neighbor or friend. Perhaps it was the ritual of the work or the chance to meditate that gave him what he so longed for but so often evaded him. Mostly he worked alone, although sometimes Barb would accompany him. Those times were about as gentle and peaceful a time as he spent with his daughter. Perhaps that is why she would accompany him. She was strong for a girl and a hard worker. Theirs was a turbulent father/daughter relationship. Barb was independent and strong willed, much like he and Mary. He knew well how she hated his drinking. He sensed how destructive his drinking had become but was not aware or could not fully understand the extent of his raging and the mistreatment and pain he inflicted on those he loved.

Frank had thought of taking up work in town as his brother and sisters did, but there was little he knew about available jobs and any he could do were not much better than what he did now. But it was steady pay. His brother

John sold gas and delivered fuel oil in the winter months and did well selling cars and was kept busy repairing them. Frank knew just how hard it was to keep a car running as his sat more often than not on blocks and in need of repairs. John was a good brother and Frank often leaned on his good nature to support his drinking habits, as well as that of his brother Mike who lived nearby.

And now even the promise of riches found in the city was dimmed by the bank failures of '29. His sisters Margaret and Josie had been hit hard for they depended on the success of business for their living. They had lost much of their life's savings when the banks failed and they couldn't be sure they would continue to have work.

Josie worked in Glenwood City for the local telephone company and with less people able to afford a telephone she was unsure how long she would have a job. Frank knew he had missed the past payments to the phone company and it was only a matter of time 'til the company would remove the batteries and put a stop to the service. Margaret worked for the Glenwood City General Store and times were equally difficult for their business too. People struggled to purchase the necessary staples of life and to pay the debts they incurred. And the store needed the funds owed to them in order to pay for new stock and the wages of their workers. Frank was among the many debtors. As a farmer much of the food they needed was raised on the farm so the family would not go hungry.

Meat and potatoes were the main course for this time of year. Frank longed for the vegetables and greens of summer. With the coming of summer they would again be a part of the daily diet. Often the kids complained about the bread and lard that had become routine at the noon meal. He barked at them in frustration whenever they complained and soon not much was said by anyone. Frank felt helpless to provide them with much more than they had and he was troubled, as he knew Mary was as well.

Stained Glass Windows

For Francis farm life was all he knew and it was nearly impossible for him to imagine much of anything else. The nearest town, Glenwood City, was about five miles distant. It was a small town with many dozens of one and two story wood buildings on either side of the main road through town and, of course, there were houses surrounding the area in close proximity to one another. It certainly did not look like any of the few pictures of cities he had seen in a book at school. Those buildings were much higher and grander than those of Glenwood City. The biggest building in Glenwood City was St. John's Catholic Church where his family attended Mass on very special occasions.

Ever since he could remember, the family made the Sunday trip, weather permitting, to attend Mass at St. Hubert's, a nearby mission church of St. John's. That was the ritual whether he or his brothers and sisters complained or not. But Francis never much complained. St. Hubert's was a mission church about a half a mile down the road from the farm, a building about as big as their barn. It sat on the east side of the road, across from the Camp 9 School, surrounded by fields and pastures about five miles to the north and west of the town of Glenwood City nestled in the hills of western Wisconsin.

Alongside the church was the cemetery and Francis had often spent time there while Dad, and sometimes his sister Barb, would work to dig a new grave for someone who had died. Francis knew about death as he had helped to drag a calf out of the barn on several occasions. It never much bothered him though. A calf was born and sometimes it got sick and died. It was a part of life on the farm. Often at church he had heard that people when they died would go to heaven or to hell. He knew heaven was a good place to go when you died and hell was not a place that anyone would want to go. Pray, behave yourself and you go to heaven he was told. Jesus loves good boys and girls. Francis didn't much think about it except for the times it was mentioned at church or when one of the farm animals died.

Rumble, bong, rumble, bong, rumble, bong, the bells of St. John's rang out. It was on one of those special occasions, quite some years ago, that Francis, after some longing looks, was granted the favor of pulling on the bell tower rope of St. John's. One of the men tugged on the rope to get it going and Francis hung on for dear life. He was a big boy for his age but he wasn't very old at the time. He was carried up and down with the momentum of the heavy bell. The pull of the rope in the pulleys overcame his weight and strength. It was as if at the first sound of the ringing of the bells, someone in the tower awoke and started pulling with you and then against you. Up and down 'til the muscles of his arms soon fatigued. Mercifully the mechanical process slowed and the bell's clappers no longer hit upon their bronze sides. The momentum of the bells finally died. Francis' heart was pounding and he felt as though he had just lost a jostling match on the living room floor with his older brother Lawrence. "Just the right amount of ring from the bells," he was told by the bell ringer.

Francis soon found and took his place near the back of the church in pews beside his Ma, sisters and younger brothers. The family was not registered as members of St. John's but of St. Hubert's. They took whatever pews were available, usually near the back or sometimes in the balcony where the choir assembled. His father and older brother Lawrence sat with the men in pews on the other side of the church.

Just as at St. Hubert's, friends, relatives and neighbors gathered from all around the countryside, but almost always the same ones and each in their own spaces. Once in a while cousins or friends would switch places or strangers would arrive and seating changes would be made but most times seating was much the same. A young man dressed in robes would appear through the door near the altar and light candles, sometimes just a couple and sometimes a dozen or more. The mass would begin soon after the candles were lit. And the multitude seemed to gather with great intensity just before the Father made his entrance. Floorboards creaked, pews filled and then all was quiet.

Candles sat in ornate holders on an equally ornate altar set against the backdrop of the sanctuary wall. The windows of the church mesmerized Francis with their beauty, color and light. They were filled with figures, some in the clouds others standing with faces looking up to the clouds. 'Had they been daydreamers too?' he wondered. There was so much about God and prayer and church that Francis did not understand.

Young boys and men carrying candles and the crucifix would begin the walk down the center aisle in procession followed lastly by the Father with robes flowing. They would stop, genuflect just inside the communion rail and take their places on padded kneelers along the steps leading to the altar. It was a majestic scene. Making a sign of the cross, the Father began "In Nomine Patris et Fillii et Spiritus Sancti, Amen" (In the name of the Father and the Son and the Holy Spirit, Amen.). This opening prayer was about all Francis understood for it accompanied a hand and arm gesture that was familiar to him. Mother would gather Francis and his brothers and sisters every night for prayer. Francis had been taught this special prayer, for what seemed to a boy of nine years of age, a very long time ago. It was a daily ritual for as long as he could remember.

Francis was glad when all of the candles were glowing for he knew the sound of the organ and voices of the choir would carry beautiful music to all who had ears to hear. The Kyrie, the Gloria; Francis loved the sound of the music, the blend of voices, the softness and the loudness. Ma would always tell them to be quiet and listen to the music and pray when they were in church. "God will speak to your heart." Most all the mass prayers were in a language Francis did not understand and if he asked his mom while in church about it her reply was a quick and stern, "shush!"

Latin, perhaps it is God's language but no one seemed really to know or at least they never said much about it. There was a certain rhythm to it all. Francis tried as best he could to listen and in his mind talk to God, Jesus, Mary or one of the saints. Sometimes he wondered why they did not speak to him. Maybe he thought he needed to be more perfect, but one thing for sure, he wouldn't give up. Someday God would talk to him. It was kind of a question and a mystery to Francis really, but outside of church he never thought much about it.

He thought however, of the saint whose name he was given, Francis. Now there was someone he might be able to understand. A friend to the animals, birds and all living things he was told. There was the story of the mean wolf that terrorized a village many years ago in a far off land. The people hearing of the good saint sent for him. The kindness of Francis changed the mean wolf into one of gentleness. Perhaps there was hope that Dad could someday be gentle too. Sometimes when he heard him yelling in anger Francis thought of the story. He longed for gentleness, kindness and love. Francis could relate to a saint like Francis.

Everyday around the farm birds sang out in greeting. All kinds of birds. Meadowlarks on a fence post sang such a melodic tune and often on an afternoon from the distant woods came the call of the bobwhite. And with the setting of the sun came the call of whippoorwills from deep within the woods and sometimes the hoot of an owl could be heard.

While Barb, Lawrence and Cele took care of the milking of the ten or so cows Francis, though younger, did chores as best he could. Often he would find himself standing by the barn door, looking out over the countryside, watching the clouds and he would notice the subtle changes of morning into day or day into night. Francis noticed changes in the air, the breezes that blew, colors of the sky, the smells and subtleties of the natural world that surrounded him. Summer was often hot and the smells of the barn were seldom subtle. Sweat rolled down his large forehead as Francis freshened the straw in the stalls or tossed hay to the cattle.

The Jackelen Homestead
This photograph was taken around the time of the death of Francis

Theirs was a smaller farm with a few small fields, a poor farm by most standards of the time. Much of the land was partially cleared pasture and thick woods. At any given time there were about eight to ten milking cows, a bull and of course, horses. There were always chickens on the loose and at times there were a few hogs, ducks or geese and always plenty of cats and a dog or two. Seldom was there a calf more than a few days old as Dad would sell the calf as soon as he found a buyer. Dad would then go off leaving Ma and the kids to the daily chores. Francis felt a certain sense of loss with Dad gone but life was more relaxed and full of laughter when he was away, especially for his older sisters and brother.

It was they and most especially his sister Barb and Lawrence who often felt the wrath of Dad. It seemed as though they paid for all of his failures. He was stern and demanding and if the cows were not milked or the chores not done just so, he was quick to go into a rage. Ben and Ralph, well they were just young kids and always seemed to be happy and free.

Tall Timothy Hay

Unhappiness hovered over Frank like a dark cloud. Life for him seemed tough except perhaps for the times when he was partying with the boys or when neighbors, friends and family gathered for a dance on a Sunday afternoon. Often the dances were held in the large loft of a barn and sometimes in the loft of a newly built barn as more land was cleared for farming. Most of the time, the parties were held at his brother Mike's not more than a mile away. It was a popular place as Mike always had plenty of good home brew. Mike, one of Francis' uncles, was a brother to Dad. Aunt Lizzie was Ma's sister. Between the two families there were seventeen in all and when a dozen or more families of relatives, friends and neighbors came together it was like a small town gathering.

Dad played the fiddle and liked to sing. His voice was strong and he knew well the songs from his childhood and the land where his pa and ma were born. Francis knew some of grandpa's and grandma's stories, and the songs too, but very little about their homeland of Germany except that it lay somewhere across a big ocean. They had sailed in a big ship many years ago and settled with families and friends amid the rolling hills of western Wisconsin. Sometimes he tried to imagine what it was like to sail a ship on the big ocean. Francis had heard that the ships were bigger than a barn. For Francis that was very big. One of his favorite songs Dad sang was "My Bonnie" and it would set his thoughts for the ocean. The love stuff of the song didn't much interest a young lad of nine. But the ocean, now that was adventure.

These gatherings were among the happiest of times for Francis and his brothers and sisters. There were lots of good things to eat and lots of boys and girls his age with whom to play. Hide and seek was a favorite game and children ran and played into the night until one by one families and friends said their good-byes and headed home for the night.

There were horses and buggies but more and more cars were the favorite means of travel. Dad had a car but it seldom ran so most often travel for Francis and his family was in a horse drawn buggy or wagon. Dad was almost always pretty liquored up when the family finally climbed into the buggy or wagon and left for home. It didn't much matter if Dad was slow on the reins for the horses, Fanny and Blackie knew the way and pretty much went on their own. It took money to keep a car going and money was something Dad had very little of. That Dad most often traveled with horses was for him and the family a good thing. There was no forgiveness in a car and Francis had seen the result of missed turns more than a time or two.

Perhaps the closest Francis felt to Dad was when Francis accompanied him to the hay fields of mid-summer. Tall Timothy grasses waved in the summer's warm breeze, nearly up to Francis' chest. Dad with a light shirt and coveralls took the scythe from his shoulder; the blade glistened as he swung it down. Francis marveled at his strength and stamina as he worked in the field cutting hay with the scythe. He would cut the field of hay in just a few days or so. Francis carried fresh water to Dad as the summer sun beat down and he kept on swinging, a swath of hay laid flat for each swing of the scythe. His large strong hands wrapped on the grips of the scythe handle, the long curved blade flowed forward and back again in steady repetition like the pendulum on grandpa and grandma's clock. To watch him at work with the scythe reminded Francis of the swooping flight of martens feeding on the summer's evening insects.

The hay fields were alive with butterflies, grasshoppers and beetles and Francis spent hours chasing them. Francis would work up a sweat just chasing a butterfly or capturing a grasshopper in the palm of his hand. He would go sit for a while in the shade of a tree and ponder the life of the grasshopper in the confines of his hand. Bringing his hands close to his eyes, he opened them slightly and peered into the darkness inside. As his eyes quickly adjusted to the dimness, he marveled at the life that lay within. How the legs folded, the many small details of its body and limbs, the eyes and the antennae. In the confine and darkness of his hand the grasshopper sat, motionless. Then Francis would open his hands and the grasshopper leapt to the freedom of the grass.

Francis thought of the stories he had heard about the swarms of hungry grasshoppers that had come and gone in years past and of the damage to crops that they caused. Francis always let the grasshoppers go for to him they were just one part of the many wonders that he observed every day. He enjoyed the summer months free from the daily ritual of school. Suddenly, as if he had just awoken, Francis ran to the shade of a nearby tree where he had placed the water jug. He looked up to see Dad still working in the hot sun. He looked down to see the jug, half full of water, just as he had left it. How long had he been sitting and daydreaming he wondered. He ran to Dad to offer some water.

Dad stopped the motion of the scythe, wiping the sweat from his face, took the jug and lifting it to the sky drank the remaining water and handed the jug back without a word. He then lifted the blade of the scythe and reaching inside one of the many pockets of his coveralls pulled out a stone. He ran the stone along the edge of the blade for a time. Putting the stone back into his pocket he reached in a smaller left side chest pocket. There was a circle of wear for it was the place of residence for the tin boxes that contained Dad's chewing tobacco. He turned open the lid and took a wad of the dark cake-like stuff and put it in his mouth. Closing the tin he put it back, secure in the pocket. Taking the grips of the scythe in his large, strong hands he went back to work.

Francis, with jug in hand, started back for the house. Francis glanced back at Dad. It was a wonder to Francis as he watched him swing the scythe in the hot summer sun.

Ma was scrubbing clothes on the washboard as he neared the house. Several lines of clothes hung drying in the breeze. Francis noticed the few little outfits belonging to his new baby brother hanging on the line. The little baby lay in the shade of one of the maple trees close to where Ma was washing. Francis' little brother Val lay fast asleep as he stooped to take a look at him. Though it was quite warm even in the shade he was wrapped in a light blanket and seemed content and quite comfortable. Ma said that Barb and Cele had gone picking berries and asked how Dad was doing with the cutting of the hay but she kept right on working. The question was one of politeness and Ma seemed quite the same whether Francis answered or not.

Barb and Cele had been helping Ma most of the morning. They had headed for the woods to pick raspberries and black-caps that were ripening. They would be a wonderful treat for dessert later this evening and Ma would can many of them to enjoy in the middle of the winter. Lawrence enjoyed the berries but hated trekking in the woods and decided that the barn could use a good cleaning. There was always so much to do.

Francis wrestled with Ben and Ralph for a while as he often did. They kicked a ball around for a while too. Francis knew he had better not dally too long as Dad would be looking for water soon. He took the dipper from the water pail that sat on the porch table. Laying it down Francis got a fresh pail of water for Ma and filled the water jug for Dad. Off again he went to the hay field with water.

Francis, "Jack" by many who knew him, was named after his father and so the nickname helped to differentiate him from Dad. He liked the nickname and it was quite appropriate as the name was derived from the first four letters of his last name. Another name, and Francis did not like it, was "Clown." He was teased about having such an extraordinarily large head making him appear rather ungainly and awkward. Francis was often teased by the neighbor kids at play, even at times by cousins, brothers and sisters uncomfortable and embarrassed by how others looked and reacted to him. When he stumbled or fell at play, "Francis the clown," was often the call. Francis went about the play and usually it was forgotten and most times never an issue. And when it was all too much for him to hear, he went to the house for the comfort and acceptance always provided by Ma.

Ma was almost always busy about something and usually kept at her work while Francis spilled out his lamentations and troubles. Sometimes Francis wondered if Ma was even listening but when Francis finished she would come to his side, putting a free arm around him, bend down, sometimes kiss his forehead and let Francis know that she loved him and what a special boy he was. Ma would give him a fresh baked treat, a piece of candy or a peanut butter cookie, Francis' favorite. Sometimes she would get a penny or two stashed in one of her many hiding places. She'd tell Francis to put it in a special place and bring the coins with him next time he was in town. "You always work so hard," she would say and Francis soon forgot about feeling bad. Once in a while though, he got a few words from Ma about toughing it out and being a big boy. Those times when Ma didn't seem to care were few but when they happened it bothered Francis quite a lot. Somehow being a big boy was not of much interest to him and he thought about how tough it must be to grow up.

Francis helped Ma often in the garden, pulling weeds, picking beans, peas or doing most of the time what Ma asked of him. Ma would be bent over with her brimmed straw hat hoeing away. She kept a steady pace for there were many rows of vegetables to care for. Often it was hot and dry and the dirt was crusty, hard and cracked, looking like so many broken dishes. He especially liked picking strawberries for he loved to eat them and in the late fall digging the potatoes which he also enjoyed eating.

Ma made the best mashed potatoes with lots of butter and milk. 'She was a good cook' Francis thought and seldom was anyone really hungry. Toward the end of winter though the diet was pretty limited as the vegetables and potatoes were pretty much gone and what was left was spoiling. Ma made the best of it though. Sometimes when times were leaner than usual and the cupboards were nearing empty, Ma made sandwiches of bread and lard. There seemed always to be enough of the lard for those yucky sandwiches. Sometimes when he was hungry they somehow tasted okay if the lard was good and was not rancid. Francis didn't much like it but when he was hungry at least it filled his stomach and eased the hunger.

Ma always hid what little money she ever had from Dad. Whenever he had a little money, he left for town and might be gone for several days or more. The family was glad for the many hiding places Ma had and for the meager amount of money she was somehow able to save. There would always be enough it seemed for flour, salt and sugar when she went to town. Ma baked bread, buns or rolls several times a week and Francis never tired of the smell of fresh bread. And once in a while for special treats Ma made sugar and peanut butter cookies and sometimes a pie or two. For a very rare and special wintertime treat she mixed sugar in cream and with a bit of vanilla and made ice cream. Ma was always secretive about the sugar and yeast. It would suddenly appear on the counter and then just as suddenly be gone.

Sometimes Ma went for her store of sugar or yeast and it would be gone. Dad was at it again. Sugar was a necessary ingredient for making brew. He drank brew far too much. He often stumbled about the house knocking over dishes breaking them on the floor. Sometimes in his unsteadiness Dad knocked over chairs or he might fall over and break what little furniture there was. Francis knew well the strength of his Dad and knew he could be very mean when he was in an unsteady state. Most of the time Francis kept his distance. Sometimes Dad was so mean that Francis was afraid. A few times he had hit Ma and tore at her dress. Sometimes he would collapse, unable to get up and lying there, fall asleep.

Blue Skies Beckon

The bright blue of an October sky excites the eye. Life is very much like October's blue, so vivid, so intense and incredibly precious. Leaves of the maples, yellows and red-oranges contrasted and intensified the blue of the sky so deep. Long before he was ever aware, a young boy would look up at the sky and take in the joy of a fleeting moment, as only the young seem able to do.

For Francis, this is where a young man should be on a day like today, not in the confines of the one room schoolhouse. On a day like today what was so important to be learned in the pages of books? For Francis the warmth of the autumn sun, the gentle breeze was all he needed to know for the moment.

What tall grasses remained, now dry and brittle, folded and crumpled beneath the quick steps of his youthful stride. Most of the pasture grasses, trimmed short by the grazing of cattle and horses remained green and fresh, still growing to reach the stage of maturity they would never know. Unlike the grasses that had grown to seed, they gave life and rejuvenated the earth in other ways. Fanny ripped another mouthful of grass and looked up to see Francis heading her way.

With the lead for Fanny in hand, Francis hurried along hurdling and sidestepping the rock, stubble and dried manure of the pasture. He bounded with the grace and ease of his youth. And two of his younger brothers followed. Francis' older sister Barb had not been feeling well and remained home from school this day. Francis walked the two miles to school most every day with Barb, his sister Cele and his brother Lawrence. They were all older, each a year older than the next. Francis seized the opportunity afforded by the change in the morning ritual and begged to stay home with his sister Barb. And he pleaded his case for he could certainly be of help with the work to be done on this bright October day. Freedom was granted.

Earlier that morning Francis had left the morning chill of the house and headed for the relative warmth of the cattle in the barn. He had scraped the manure, fed the hay and helped Cele and Lawrence who did the milking. After chores were done he returned to a house transformed by the warmth of the oven and the wonderful aroma of fresh baked bread. Ma buttered a slice of the still warm bread and gave one to Cele and Lawrence who were now walking their way to school. Cele loved school and was smart. Lawrence, like Francis, didn't much like school. He had a hard time with his studies but most of the time it was better than staying at home with Dad.

Dad was muttering to Ma about Barb being sick again. "Achhh, she's just lazy and doesn't want to work." Turning to Francis, "As long as you're going to be around then there are potatoes to be dug." Dad ordered, "Go on now" and he sat down at the table and began downing a breakfast of several eggs and a pile of potatoes fried in and glistening with bacon grease, the usual fare. While Francis looked for his jacket and gloves Ma in silence went about her work in the kitchen. She buttered the golden crust of the rolls she

had removed from the warm pan. Ma tore a freshly buttered bun from the corner and handed it to Francis as he left
the house for the garden.

The October morning was crisp and the sky clear and
blue. The light frost of the morning was gone with the rising of the sun. Francis took the fork from the ground and
began to dig. There were numerous rows to be done and for
now Francis enjoyed the task. He'd dig into a hill and lift its
treasure from the earth. He'd bounce the fork and the dirt
fell away. The potatoes remained and he dumped them into
a pile. Later, he would toss them into a gunnysack and so
the process went.

Sometime later Ma appeared with Val wrapped up snug
in blankets. She lay a blanket down and placed Val upon it.
She then joined him in the garden for there was a lot to do.
Francis was helping Ma as they bagged the potatoes when
Dad hollered for Francis. Francis and Ma knew that Dad
was fixing to head to town again. Dad probably wanted
some help with the wagon or hitching the horses and Francis liked nothing more than to please his father.

Francis understood and knew his father well. The morning before a nice heifer calf had been born and, as was his
ritual, Dad would load her up and take it to town. The few
dollars it was worth would go to Dad. A piece of candy perhaps would be all he and his brothers and sisters would see
if Dad was in a kindly way. Francis, although only a young
boy of nine did many things, some of which only a man
should do, as did many boys his age. Francis had gone for
Fanny so many times before.

Francis lay down the potato fork and headed across the
garden to where Dad was working on the wagon alongside the barn. Ma kept filling the gunnysack with the newly
dug potatoes. When he came to the edge of the garden he
stopped, turned and looked at Ma bent over, filling the potato sack. He looked and could sense the sadness in her heart.
He turned again and left her alone to work in the garden.

Francis headed off to the barn. Eight months old, Val, his new baby brother lay in blankets on the grass at the edge of the garden. A kind of makeshift playpen surrounded him. Francis picked Val up and kissed his forehead as his mother had done for him so many times before. Eyes, bright and blue smiled back at Francis as he gently put him down and headed to the barn.

Dad was replacing a floorboard that had rotted away on the wagon that sat outside the barn. "Go get that lazy damn horse," Dad ordered Francis. Dad's mind was on getting the calf loaded up and making for town to get what he could for the calf. Most of the proceeds would go to replenish his liquor supplies. Frank would pay a debt here and part of one there and would take on more debt someplace else. It wasn't always easy to get what he needed with the little money he had. Fanny was still in the pasture while Blackie had already come in for water and was now in the barn. He entered the barn and pulled the lead from the wall and headed out the barn for the pasture and Fanny.

Ralph and Ben, who had been playing hide and seek in the barn, followed close behind Francis. Francis enjoyed their company most of the time. Sometimes they were annoying as he was to his older sisters and brother. Today they played touch tag as they headed to the pasture where Fanny grazed.

Arms Of Love

Fanny was a mare, a good strong workhorse, but she was lazy. She was a favorite riding horse and if a young rider slipped or fell from her back she would immediately stop, stand still and calmly wait for her rider to climb up and on her back again. Fanny was white as clover blossoms in summer with a flowing white mane to match. She was enjoying the pasture on this bright October morning and like Francis, enjoying her freedom.

Fanny would be a challenge today for she had caught sight of Francis and the lead rope he carried. He knew however once the lead snapped in place she would go back to the barn quiet and calm. Fanny, her mane flowing against the deep blue sky of this October morning, disappeared over a rise and into a back corner of the pasture. A corn binder stood on a crest of hill nearby. Francis, using the corn binder as a blind, waited. His younger brothers Ben and Ralph were closer now, chasing one another from behind one tree and then another laughing and playing a simple game as only children know how to do. And Francis and Fanny were playing their own game too.

Finally as Francis got closer to Fanny he waited for just the right moment, to reach for her halter and to snap the lead in place. However, Fanny quickly turned and eluded Francis several times. Ben and Ralph watched as Francis made his attempts. Ralph knew that he could approach Fanny and would be greeted with a gentle nuzzle. "Give the lead to me," Ralph insisted. Francis, a bit jealous of his younger brother's friendship with Fanny gave him the lead. Ralph walked up to Fanny and snapped the lead in place. With the lead in hand Ralph began to walk to the barn.

Dad would be happy Francis thought for it hadn't taken too long. As they neared the barn however, Fanny turned and pulling the lead from Ralph's hand ran for the far side of the pasture. They again hiked out to the pasture. Ralph approached Fanny and grabbed the lead dangling from the halter. Once again as they neared the barn Fanny stopped, turned and pulled the lead from Ralph's hand.

And again the three boys headed to the far pasture where Fanny waited among the trees as if playing a game of hide and seek. Ralph approached Fanny who stood calm and still as always. Ralph again grabbed the lead. Francis insisted now that Ralph hand him the lead since he had lost

Fanny twice already. He would take Fanny to the barn and this time she would not run away. Ralph reluctantly gave the lead to Francis. Fanny, nuzzling Francis, stood calmly munching on the grass while Francis tied the lead loosely around his waist.

As Francis led the way, he thought how enjoyable it was to lead Fanny to the barn with hands that were free. He would pull at what was left of the straggles of long Timothy that grew among the thistle or by the numerous sun dried cow pies that dotted the pasture providing fertilizer for the grasses of the seasons to come. Offering the gift within his hand to Fanny, he kept a prime strand of the Timothy to chew on. The juice of the grass was pleasant to taste and a custom he was introduced to when just a young boy.

Suddenly Francis heard a noise from behind; as he turned to look he simultaneously heard the unmistakable sound of hooves pounding the earth and the lead around his waist dug into his sides and back. Filled with utter terror at the realization that Fanny had turned and run, Francis hit the earth hard. He grabbed for the lead. All was a blur as the gentle earth suddenly transformed into an earth Francis had never known. The peace of this October day was shattered by the violent blur and rush of brush, rock and stubble. As Francis was dragged, his hands and arms wrapped over his head, his body turned as he hit a stump.

Again and again he was turned and torn; his body seethed and was consumed in pain. Time suddenly became an eternity. And then for Francis, all was peaceful and still. Muscles pulsing in movement and rhythm Fanny continued to run. The lead frayed and cut by brush and stone, at last gave way and broke in two. With the sudden release of the pull on her head and neck Fanny stopped. Francis' body lay still beside a pine tree near the back of the pasture. Fanny, again free, lowered her head and began to tear at the grass of what remained of the late autumn pasture.

Ben and Ralph, hollering and running as fast as they could, came to the spot where Francis lay. They looked at the body of their brother as blood trickled from his head. Blood was running down a large cut on the side of his forehead. There were numerous scrapes and cuts on his arms and legs. "Wake up. Francis, wake up!!!" They kept on as if with a litany, not understanding why Francis did not move nor open his eyes. A fear they could not understand nor contain grew within them. Tears filled their eyes and Ralph began to cry. The sounds of the two boys crying out the words "Wake up, Francis, wake up" carried across the hay field and road to neighboring farms.

Ben had traveled the countryside surrounding Glenwood City for many years now. He sold Watkins products and it seemed whatever else his customers might have a hankering for. The past couple of years had been lean and often the stops he made were more about visits than about sales. Sometimes he went home with a loaf of fresh bread or part of a ham as the result of a transaction with a family with little money and in need. Sometimes he sold his product for barely more than his cost. He considered his customers his friends and faithfully made the rounds. As he turned off the road and started up the driveway he noticed Clara bent over at work in her garden. She, like many this bright October day, was gathering the harvest of what remained in her garden. He parked the car and turning the key the rumpus noise of the engine was silenced. He walked down the path to the garden.

Clara looked up and greeted Ben. The purchase of items she might need was not part of her thought for the moment. She voiced her concern regarding what she had heard just a short while earlier as she went about digging the carrots. She said, "I heard the running of a horse and the hollering of kids and I'm concerned for what might have happened. Would you be so kind as to stop by the Jackelen place? I don't want to alarm him about what may have happened so tell Frank his cows are in our fields," she said. Looking down at a bunch of newly dug carrots Clara bent down and grabbed a bunch and shaking the dirt loose handed them to Ben. "Have some carrots for your trouble Ben." "Clara, you don't have to give me anything" Ben replied. "Go on, take them now, I insist" was Clara's sharp reply. "Well then, thanks Clara" Ben replied, knowing that no amount of protest would change her mind. Walking back to the car he drove away and headed up the road.

Mary and Frank were one of his customers from which he seldom expected much of a sale. Mary most of the time had a little something she needed and he enjoyed the visits along with a bun or slice of bread. Most times the kids came running to see him and he always had a bit of candy for each of them. He turned off the main road and into the driveway of Frank and Mary. Theirs was a farm on intersecting roads. Frank was greasing a wheel on the wagon along the upper the part of the driveway leading to the side road. As he rounded the drive Ben noticed Mary, like Clara, was bent over hard at work in garden. He drove alongside the wagon. "Frank" he said, "Clara thinks your cows are in the field on the other side of the pasture." Frank thanked Ben, and muttering to himself "Damn cows anyway," headed for the crest of the hill and the pasture. Ben sat for a moment and watched as Frank headed for the pasture. As he neared the crest of the hill he saw Frank begin to run.

Francis' body lay limp, his exposed flesh cool and pale, the lead wrapped tight around his body. Ben and Ralph knelt beside him. "Come, Francis, wake up. Wake up, Francis," they cried, tears rolling down their cheeks. Fanny continued to graze a short distance away, frayed lead dragging in the grass. Dad knelt down at Francis' side. He noticed the slow almost imperceptible pulse of the artery of Francis' neck. Blood, dark, soaked parts of the ground. Francis' coat, torn nearly from his body, lay in shreds. Dad loosened the lead, carefully and gently removed it.

Ben and Ralph were quiet now, faces stained with dirt and tears. Dad held back his own tears as he slid his right arm and hand under the head and shoulders of Francis. His left hand and arm he slid under the back of Francis' knees.

Gently he cradled him close to his chest. Moving his left foot forward, raising his knee and straightening his back, with the muscles of his legs slowly he brought himself to stand. Francis now lay limp in his arms.

He was a big boy for his age but Frank in his shock and grief hardly noticed. It was his little son in his arms. 'How could he have sent a boy to do what he himself should have done?' Over and over he kept asking himself, 'Why?' And yet he knew there was no hope of an answer other than his own condemnation echoing though his head. 'How could I, how could I?' It kept going around in his head like so many circling vultures ready to devour what little remained of the shreds of his decency.

All the while Ben and Ralph watched Dad and he hadn't said a word. They weren't about to either. Ben and Ralph turned and began the walk up the sloping hill of the pasture thinking Dad would soon follow. Francis had been lying near a pine tree near the farthest edge of the pasture. A hay field separated the pasture from the nearest neighbor. The two boys, after walking only a very short way sensed their Dad was not following and turned to see where he was. He remained standing where Francis had lain. He was looking skyward. Then, lowering his head to look at Francis cradled in his arms he began to walk. 'If only it had been the cows in the field,' Frank thought. 'If only I would have gone for Fanny this would not have happened.' The pasture fence was in some disrepair. The barbed wire on the fence was hanging low and placing his boot on it he stepped over and into the field continued on. It would be a walk he would take, again and again whether he wanted to or not for many years to come. Ben and Ralph watched for a while and realizing that Dad would not be following turned around and headed for home. Ralph, a young boy of barely five years and Ben, a year and a half older, would each in their own way carry memories and the burdens that those memories would bring for the rest of their lives.

As Frank walked he looked at his son, his heart was heavy. Tears welled up in his eyes even though it had been many years since he had shed a tear. He felt the blood pulsing through his body, feeding the muscles of his arms and legs as they began to tire under the weight of the precious load they carried.

Frank prayed that somehow Francis might be healed. Prayed for a miracle he believed would not come. There were no miracles in his life. All that remained were the reminders of failures he saw wherever he looked. Even the daily toil of labor and work well done were gradually stripped of their dignity, as more and more the work remained undone. The bottle, slowly robbing him of the beauty of life and the loving touch of others, was the only healing salve he now knew. 'What would he say to Mary, for here was her son, body so badly broken, lying limp, cradled in his arms? How could she not hate me for what had happened to her son,' he thought. How he longed to take a drink, drift off into oblivion; forget the pain of this moment.

Francis could hear the singing of a meadowlark and sensed a loving presence surround him. 'Are these the arms of Jesus who was now carrying him?' Francis moaned ever so slightly. Frank mechanical-like kept walking, one foot in front of the other. Blinded by the pain within Frank did not hear the singing of the bird or feel the gentle breeze that caressed him. Nor did he know who he was, for he was lost in the deep and dark night of the soul.

Felix came out of the barn and looked out over the field as he often did taking in the last of the beautiful gold and yellows that remained in the woods beyond. His eyes caught sight of Frank. 'Something must be very wrong. Who is he carrying in his arms?' Felix wondered. As Frank neared the road he could see that it was Francis. "Jack! Jack! Oh no, not Jack" he said to himself in sudden shock of realization. He hollered to his wife in near panic "Come quickly." She came running, the screen door slamming behind. "It looks as though Jack's been hurt very badly." Felix and his wife got in the car and drove down the driveway and parked along the field. They readied the back of the seat. Frank carrying Francis, bloody, pale and limp in his arms stepped out of the tall autumn grass of the field. Felix whispered to his wife to call the doctor to the Jackelen place as he assisted Frank holding Jack into the back seat of the car.

Felix started the car and began the short drive to Jack's place. He glanced back and Jack just lay there. Frank sat saying not a word. He sat, looking out the window as the countryside passed by.

A couple of nickels jiggled in a tray near the dash. Felix thought back to the past spring and the end of the school year picnic. His own children went to school with Jack, Lawrence, Barb and Cele. Now Jack, there was a stout and strong boy for his age. Kids would line up to see who could take Jack down. But almost without exception, it was they who were taken down by Jack. Felix had a deal with Jack, a nickel for each one. And now Jack lay pale, bleeding and unconscious. Felix fought back the tears. He glanced at Frank and saw that his head had not moved. Frank too had been bloodied and broken, not by the running of a horse but by the weight of the suffering and pain.

It seemed as though he had been driving all afternoon as he turned the car into Frank and Mary's driveway. Many times he had turned into this driveway to stop for a visit or to lend a helping hand or take Mary, Frank or one of the kids to town. Always before it was with joy and gladness that he came. Today was alarmingly different. 'Mary' he thought, 'somehow I need to tell Mary, very gently though.' Felix pulled up close to the front door and stopped the car.

Barb, looking out of the kitchen window hollered to Ma, "Felix and Dad are here. Francis is in the back of the car and looks all bloody." Felix entered the house just as Mary came into the kitchen. "Don't get excited Mary but Francis is badly hurt." Mary sat down on a kitchen chair, wilted and overcome with the sudden reality of the moment, her body and soul at once awash in grief. "We'll need clean sheets on your bed," Felix said. Theirs was the only mattress in the house of any substance. The kids slept upstairs on straw-ticks, sewn material stuffed with straw. Felix entered Frank and Mary's bedroom just off the kitchen and placing clean sheets on the bed readied it for Francis. Then, with haste he returned to the car.

Frank raised Francis' back and head slightly and Felix with one arm and hand reached under Jack's head and shoulders and lifted. Frank was grateful to his friend Felix. Frank, sullen and weak, his strength spent for the moment, seemed almost confused and dazed.

Water And A Gift Of Flowers

Felix felt the warmth of the blood as it trickled down his arm. Felix now carried Jack in his arms and walked to the house. Lawrence and Cele had arrived home from school and watched as Felix arranged the limp body of their brother Francis in his arms. Lawrence opened the screen door to the porch. Cele went quickly and stood next to Ma. Mary, standing now, watched as Felix carried Francis into the bedroom and laid him gently down on the bed. Mary had poured a teakettle of warm water in a washbasin she had placed on the bedroom night stand. She followed Felix into the bedroom and sitting on the edge of the bed began washing the blood, dirt and grime from Francis' head and body. She noticed the shallowness his breathing. As she gently washed, Francis voiced a barely audible moan. "My son, my son," Mary said, and the tears flowed.

From behind the partially closed door of the bedroom Ben and Ralph looked in on Ma and Francis. Ma rinsed the cloth in the washbasin and dabbed at Francis' wounds again and again. 'Poor Francis,' Ralph thought for he knew how much he disliked the dirt rubbed off his face after a day of play. But this was something very different. She was so gentle and Francis lay there without movement. Ralph always squirmed in protest but Francis only lay there. As he watched, tears flowed from Ma's eyes, falling on Francis' face as she bent over her son. 'Perhaps with the washing,' Ralph thought, 'Francis would awaken.'

Ralph thought about Francis lying by the tree in the pasture. He and Ben had done all they could, even removing his heavy overshoes thinking it would be easier for Francis to get up. They had told him over and over again to wake up, to please wake up. 'Stubborn Francis. Stubborn, stubborn Francis,' Ralph thought, 'I could have taken the lead and Fanny would have followed but stubborn Francis wouldn't listen.' Ralph thought about what had happened, but said not a word, as he watched Ma for it might break the ritual that he thought would soon awaken Francis.

Cele took Ben and Ralph by the hand and went through the kitchen and out into the late afternoon sun. Somehow the sun did not seem as bright as Ralph left the house. Then, suddenly the sun was bright again, for Ralph heard the familiar and welcome challenge. "Last one to the windmill is a rotten potato," Cele called out and away they ran up the hill to where the windmill stood. Ralph as usual was the rotten potato and he complained a bit but it didn't much matter.

They drank of the cool water and sat down on the platform that covered the cistern. Laying down they looked up as the fluffy white clouds drifted across the sky framed by the metal support of the windmill. As he lay there, Ben thought of climbing to the top, for he loved the thrill and the view of the countryside was special from atop its perch. But with all that had happened he was tired and content right where he was for the moment. And besides, his sister would surely get upset if he started to climb.

The wood stove in the kitchen was fired up and the boiler placed on top. Felix, his wife and a neighbor worked in the kitchen tending the fire and boiler. Felix's wife, who had made a call for the doctor before coming up to lend a hand, informed Felix that the doctor was on another call but would come as soon as he could. The batteries for the phone on Frank and Mary's kitchen wall had been removed and it hung on the wall, useless. Frank had not been able to pay the bill. Josie, Frank's sister who worked for the phone company during a visit the previous day had reluctantly removed them. "Are you sure?" she asked. "We don't need the phone!" Frank had replied. Felix entered the bedroom and gently placing his hand on Mary's shoulder, bent his head down and whispered, "The doctor is on his way and will be here soon."

Barb, with little Val in her arms, sat resting her back against the side of the barn. The late afternoon rays of autumn's golden sun warmed her as she held her brother close. She hugged him tight and then looking down at his face, smiled as his eyes smiled back at hers. Val was a comfort for her now. Barb knew somehow that Jack was hurt real bad and she prayed as she sat holding her brother in her arms. She let her mind wander. Jack, Cele and herself most times slept in the same bed in the upstairs bedroom; for one or more of them often wet the bed at night and one wet bed was more than enough to take care of as far as Ma was concerned. And when Barb complained Ma would mutter there was only so much straw. Sometimes she would get so mad at Ma and she would feel bad later for she knew how hard it was for her ma each day.

Often Dad would go to town and come home drunk. Ma had threatened to leave him on a number of occasions. It had been sometime since she had made mention of that though. Barb remembered the last time she heard Ma talk of leaving him was after her First Communion and that was already four years ago. Her mind kept wandering. She wondered how Ma was doing now with Jack hurt. She looked to the house. Cele was playing with Ben and Ralph. Lawrence she knew was in the barn doing the chores as she could hear the blade scraping the manure from the walkways of the barn.

A car turned into the driveway. Aunt Josie and Aunt Margaret were here. She was comforted at the sight and got up from where she sat. She met them at the car. "How is Jack?" they asked." Barb replied she did not know as Ma had asked her to take care of Val for a while. Josie and Margaret walked to the house and Barb, carrying Val close in her arms, followed them in. Felix and his wife were busy about the kitchen but came and greeted Margaret and Josie as they entered the house. "How is Jack?" Josie asked. "Jack is hurt bad, really bad. The doctor should be here any time but for now we can only wait," replied Felix.

Ma came from the bedroom and greeted her sisters-in-law who were always so very kind and good to her. Not much was said. Ma put her arm around Barb, "Let's put Val in the cradle and see if he'll sleep for a while." As Barb carried Val to the cradle Ma followed. "Thanks Barb," she said. "Now could you go to your Aunt Lizzie's and get some Holy Water. We have none and Father will be here soon."

With a quick good-bye to her aunts Barb ran out the door and on her way. As she ran across the yard the doctor turned his car into the driveway. He was a comfort to see. 'Jack will surely be alright now' Barb thought, but she could not get rid of the nagging doubt that her brother might not get better. She gave a quick wave and the doctor smiled back at her. Uncle Mike's place was about a mile away. Barb turned up the road and ran as fast as she could.

The Holy Water was most important and it would be so embarrassing if the Father got to the house and there was none available when he asked for some. 'Poor Ma,' Barb thought, 'and with Francis hurt so badly. It might be more than she could bear.' Where that water came from she was not sure. Ma had said it was specially blessed. She often wondered if it tasted different. She just knew that it came from church in a little glass jar with a cross on it and that Aunt Lizzie had some. She was running as fast as she could to get the water so that Father would have it for her brother when he got there. Father would ask for the precious liquid of course, of that she was sure. There had been many times when Ma had sprinkled her when she was sick with a high fever as well as her sister Cele and her brothers. She always got better, so did Cele, Lawrence, Francis, Ralph and Ben. She didn't think that Ma had sprinkled Val yet as he had not got really sick as of yet. 'Francis would certainly get well' she thought 'if he could receive a sprinkling.'

Father Rivers had baptized Val about five months ago and poured water on his head. That couldn't have been the Holy Water as she was sure baptism water was just plain water. Or was it?

Many thoughts raced through her head just as fast as her legs raced over the dirt of the road. As she continued to run, she remembered how she had still been angry with her brother only this morning. She must somehow seek her brother's forgiveness when she returned. Suddenly the thought occurred that she might have been the last one to be sprinkled with Ma's Holy Water and that because of her there was now none. And Francis needed it so very much. Perhaps it is the only thing in the world that could make her brother better.

Her side was beginning to hurt now and she held her right hand there as she continued to run. Uncle Mike and Aunt Lizzie's place was just a short distance ahead. She slowed her pace but kept running. As she arrived in the yard her cousins ran to meet her and were full of questions. Had they heard already? She didn't stop to answer but ran up the steps and opened the door. "Francis is hurt really bad and Ma has no Holy Water left." Lizzie turned and left the kitchen and just as quickly returned bottle in hand. Aunt Lizzie already knew of the accident. "We'll be there just as soon as we can" she said and handed the precious liquid to Barb. Barb gave her aunt a quick hug and out the door she ran. Her cousins asked if she could stay and play. "Not now but maybe we can later," Barb replied already a bit breathless. Across the lawn she ran out onto the road.

Her side was already hurting again. Holding the precious liquid tight in her hand perhaps she would have to slow the pace now. And she surely would not want to trip and fall, breaking the bottle and spilling its contents upon the dirt of the road. She slowed down to a fast walk, mixing the pace with occasional running. She would soon be home and Ma would be so happy to see that she had brought the Holy Water. She only hoped that the Father would not be there when she arrived. Her mind continued to race even though her legs had slowed. She at last reached the rise of the road and just ahead was the intersection of the side road with the main road. The run was easier now and as she reached the intersection Barb cut straight for the house. She looked for the Father's car. It wasn't there and she slowed to a walk and caught her breath. The doctor's car was still there but he was walking to the car. He placed his bag behind his seat, got into the car, drove down the driveway turning onto the main road and heading toward town. 'Perhaps Jack was doing better now' Barb thought.

Aunt Margaret and Aunt Josie's car was still there as was Felix's and his wife's and there were now a couple of more cars along the driveway. One of the neighbors was bringing the cows into the barn. Ben and Ralph were at play in a pile of leaves with a couple of neighbor kids, enjoying the warmth and lingering light of the autumn sun.

Barb entered the kitchen. The house seemed uncommonly quiet, and there was less commotion than when she had left just a while ago. Cele was holding Val. Felix was bringing in wood for the stove. Josie and Margaret were sitting in the parlor in hushed conversation. 'Perhaps that was good,' Barb thought. Barb looked in the bedroom. The room was darkened with gathered curtains but rays of light found their way through the folds and created a pattern of light and shadow. The crucifix that hung on the wall alongside the bed was now set on the night stand with two unlit candles and a small white cloth. Ma was standing looking down at Jack. His head was now bandaged in strips of cloth.

He looked as if he was an angel, pale and motionless. The scene was alien and troubled Barb. "Ma, here's the Holy Water." Barb whispered to her. Without a word Ma took the bottle in her hands, and clasping them tight, brought them close to her bosom. Ma's lips began to move, in the faint whispering of the familiar ritual of prayer as she sprinkled her son with droplets of the precious liquid.

Barb turned and left the bedroom. Cele was still holding Val and she stood looking at her sister and brother for a moment in silence. 'Was Cele thinking some of the same things she was thinking?' Barb wondered.

All Barb wanted was for Jack to get better. She needed to ask his forgiveness. Francis had made her so angry at times with his many antics. Just the other day she was playing house in the as yet empty corn crib and he came and took her doll away. Barb had given chase and caught Francis but in the tussle ripped the fabric of the doll's arm. Barb was so angry. This morning after breakfast he brought her some petunias and some seeds as a gesture of peace. As Francis worked with Ma in the garden she soon tossed them aside.

'Why did I have to think about what had happened this morning on the run for the water?' she thought. She had not run purely for love of her brother. There was also the embarrassment of not having the Holy Water when Father Rivers would arrive and she wanted most desperately to do what she could to help her mother. But she really did love Francis though, as she did all her brothers and her sister. The feelings of her shadowed anger were still there and guilt welled within. Now she found herself in search of that gift she had so casually discarded in the tall autumn grass.

There the flowers lay just as she had tossed them. Tears filled her eyes as she looked upon them and managed a smile. Closing her eyes for a moment she could see her brother sheepishly carry them to her. "I picked these just for you" he had said and placed them in her hands. He did not say anything about her doll, somehow words were not important and Francis had a hard time with words. He had felt bad about the incident though and in his usual manner sought peace through forgiveness. She forgave him, though she had not said a word to him and at that moment had not realized the preciousness of the gift he had given to her.

She scooped them up in her hands ever so carefully. They were wilted and lifeless, having been separated from the life giving water that fed them for nearly a day. They at once reminded her of her brother lying in Felix's arms as he carried him in the house not long ago. Carefully she carried them to the house, filled a vase with water and placed the stems of the flowers into the vase and sat them on a table alongside the bed in which she, Cele and Jack most usually slept. The flowers drooped over the sides of the vase. "There Francis. I do forgive you" she whispered to herself and walked out of their upstairs bedroom.

Family And Friends

Mike and Lizzie drove in and parked to the side not far from the wagon Frank had been working on earlier in the day. Ben and Ralph, seeing them, ran to the car and were there before the engine could sputter to a halt. "Uncle Mike! Aunt Lizzie!" together they chorused. "I think something is wrong with Francis," the younger Ralph blurted out in excitement. "Fanny, she kept running. Francis didn't let go. He was hurt and won't talk to us now." Ralph hung his head looking down at the ground. "If only I would have taken the lead she wouldn't have run. I told Francis I could do it, I told him. Fanny wouldn't have run on me." Lizzie took Ralph in her arms. "Ralph, come now, don't be blaming yourself, you're just a little boy. There was nothing a little boy like you could have done. Horses sometimes get spooked and they run." She assured him she would check on Francis and see what she could do. Lizzie looked at Ben standing more quietly than usual, his eyes fixed on the distance of the countryside. "Ben," Lizzie put her arm around him, "It's good to see you."

Lizzie began to wonder just how badly Francis was hurt. Cele arrived to greet Lizzie and Mike. "Francis is hurt very bad" she whispered to Lizzie out of concern for her younger brothers. "The doctor went to town to get his wife and more supplies from his office. He'll be back soon. It will be good for Ma to see you." Cele took Ralph by the hand. "Come on Ralph; let's see if we can find a place where Ben can't find us." Ben gave Cele a nod and away they ran. Standing by his aunt for a moment Ben finally spoke up. "Where's Will?" Lizzie replied,"He's at home doing chores but I'll tell him hello for you Ben." "Thanks Aunt Lizzie" and Ben trotted away to find where Cele and Ralph were hiding.

Mike stood quietly next to Lizzie. In many ways Mike was like his brother Frank and Lizzie much like her sister Mary Together Lizzie and Mike slowly made their way up to the house. Margaret came outside to greet them. Eyes and silence spoke with a deafening roar as together they entered the house. Mary, knowing of Lizzie's arrival, was there to meet her. Eyes met and sisters embraced, a treasured gift only understood by sisters. Sisters who have shared their lives with one another, carried with them in the innermost regions of their beings the times of their youth, the deepest of feelings freely given and shared with one another in the moments of their most desperate need.

Together they entered the bedroom. Francis lay, motionless, wounds wrapped with the tenderness of love's caring and compassion. The stillness amplified the shallowness of his breathing. Lizzie gazed upon her nephew and took his hand. It was warm and still within her hand. Laughter and the sounds of children at play echoed in her mind and for a moment seemed to bounce even from the walls of the room. Lips moved and whispered in prayer.

People gathered in various rooms of the house, whispering, breaking into the stillness of waiting. "Why hasn't the doctor taken him to a hospital?" "Would he not be able to better care for Francis there?" "There must be something more he could do or does he figure rest is all he needs?" Family and friends continued to come and go as the evening wore on. Some had noticed Fanny standing nearby the house, rubbing her neck on a corner of the house. They wondered about how the accident happened. Some questioned the wisdom of sending a child to do a man's work. How and why had Fanny, the gentlest of horses, and most nearly a family pet, been spooked? Some people wondered and searched for answers and still others remained quiet, listening, nodding and praying for the acceptance for themselves and Jack's family of what would be. As word spread, the thoughts and prayers of many filled the evening air as the bright blue of that October day fused into the golden light of the setting sun. The hearts and hands of many friends and relatives filled the house with their care and concern and offered, in whatever humble ways, were hope and support.

Love Fills A Home

The house again hushed as the doctor and his wife returned. They nodded to Felix and to those that had gathered and entered the bedroom. The doctor's wife carried within her arms new cloth that would dress the wounds of the young Francis. Mary and Lizzie stood in silent waiting and prayer. The doctor, opening his bag, took the stethoscope, warming the cone in his hands for a moment. He then gently pulled the covers from Francis' chest and moved the instrument over it, pausing, listening, pausing and listening again and again, his face and expression frozen as if time had suddenly vanished and was no longer a concern. He at last looked into the eyes of Mary and he could not hide from his own eyes what he knew would be only a matter of time. "Mary. We will clean and wrap Francis' wounds in new dressings. It shouldn't take too long. Perhaps you should go and sit down and rest for a while."

Val had been fussing and went from arm to arm over the last hour or so. Lizzie took Mary's hand and together they left the room. Mary took Val, cradled him in her arms and went upstairs to nurse. She sat in the chair with Val nuzzled to her breast and began nursing her baby boy There was comfort for her in this act of love. The baby she held was all the more precious and she gently ran her fingers through his hair.

She thought of Francis whom she held close not so many years before and of the lullabies she knew. Softly she began to hum and then ever so softly to sing. Soon, content, Val fell fast asleep in her arms. She got up from the rocking chair and laid him gently in the cradle. She tucked the covers around him and sat back down in the chair, placing her crossed hands to her heart as if she again caressed her Francis in her arms. She began to rock, to hum and then sing, ever so softly and sweetly for her little boy who lay on her bed so wounded. It was as if with the gift of her music she was singing the young boy unto heavenly rest. The strength of her faith was her consolation and the means by which she would let go of the life she had nurtured for such a short time.

Memories filled her heart. Mary thought of the day Francis accompanied her to town to do some shopping. There was a man who had no feet or legs just below the knees. He rode a platform of sorts on wheels and scooted about the town. Francis upon seeing him asked, "Did God run out of clay when he made him Ma?" She smiled at him and her heart was glad that he listened to the stories of a faith so dear and so close to her heart. It was a brief moment but Mary entered into the peace of that moment.

Felix had brought warm water to the doctor and his wife who began to remove the cloth from Francis' head. Gently they raised his head from the pillow to unwrap the cloth. They did so quietly in synchronized movement from having worked together many years now. Ever so carefully the last layers were removed. Gently she dabbed at the blood that had dried beneath the cloth. The doctor began placing ointment on the wounds of Francis' head. The doctor's wife now saw for herself the futility of a hospital bed. The wound was severe and there would be no recovery for this young boy. These were the times her husband's skill could not change the stark reality of what was to come. She watched and wondered at the depth of his dedication and the inner strength and spirit that sustained him in moments like these. He was a healer and did much for so many. She had seen it time and again in their many years together. Sometimes it seemed almost miraculous.

This time the healing touch of her husband's hands would be reflected back to him by his simple act of caring. It was as though Francis who lay so still, so wounded would do the healing and give her husband the strength to carry on and to heal again those in need of his care. Together the doctor and his wife wrapped the head of Francis with the clean cloth. Again he placed the stethoscope to Francis' chest. He listened and wondered 'How long?' He packed his bag and left the room. They entered the kitchen and a basin was filled with warm water for them.

With a start Mary woke. With suddenness the reality and pain returned. Mary got up from the chair and for a moment stood bent over the cradle. She watched as Val's little chest raised and lowered in the rhythm of his breathing. Mary turned and headed for the top of the stairway. Slowly, deliberately she made her way down.

The doctor was washing his hands in the kitchen basin when Mary walked in. Drying his hands on a towel he walked over to Mary. "Come with me Mary and see your son." They walked to the side of the bed where Francis lay peaceful and still. "Mary, you know don't you? It's only a matter of time. Francis may not live through this night. There is not much more I can do for him."

"Thank you for all that you and your wife have done," Mary replied. "If there is anything else I can do for you Mary please get word to me," the doctor replied. Tears welled in her eyes as the doctor left the room and Mary stood alone watching her son as he lay in her bed. The doctor entered the kitchen, he and his wife said their good-byes and left. Lizzie again joined her sister and the house was filled with family and friends. Their care and concern were a gift to her and would sustain her now and in the days to come.

Frank and Mike leaned against Mike's car. The doctor's car was alongside it. Frank, his head bowed, gazed at the ground. Hearing the screen door shut he looked up as the doctor came toward him. Frank walked to meet him, eyes pleading for that glimmer of hope that eluded him. "I'm sorry Frank. There is nothing I can do for your son." The doctor offered his hand. Frank took the doctor's hand into his. Frank's hand, always so strong and vibrant, seemed weak and trembling as if grasping for some energy to renew again the strength and life it had lost. The doctor looked into Frank's eyes and steel blue eyes betrayed the deep sorrow and the reality of what Frank was now facing.

Good Night Little Brother

The family waited for the priest, Father Rivers, who would be arriving shortly. It wasn't long before his car entered the drive. Aunt Margaret met him as he made his way to the house. Margaret filled him in on what the doctor had said as she escorted the priest into the bedroom.

Family gathered around, watching, waiting and praying. The Holy Water Barb had so dutifully brought earlier in the day sat upon the table with the crucifix and candles. The candles were lit. Taking the stole from his pocket the priest draped it around his neck and removing the little book of prayers and placing a jar of Holy Oil on the white cloth of the table he began the prayers and readings for the Sacrament of the Last Rite. "In Nomine Patris et Fillii et Spiritus Sancti, Amen." The Latin that poured forth was sure and direct, the anointing of the head and the hands with the oil, deliberate and light of touch. Mary and Frank stood quiet and still, intently watching, waiting for the miracle they hoped would be theirs. The priest continued to pray from the book of prayers and with a final "Amen" again there was silence.

Francis lay there as if asleep, still, but for the barely perceptible movement of his diaphragm in breathing and the slow pulsing of the veins in his neck. The priest stood silent as he gazed on the now nearly lifeless young lad he had seen so many times sitting in the pews with his mother and siblings at Sunday Mass.

'Dear God,' he thought, 'How do I help them to let go? What do I say, words, how futile. German, English, Latin?' For himself, at a time like this Latin was somehow easier. Through the years he had grown comfortable with it as it was the language of his prayer life. He knew it was a place in which he took refuge at times like these. There would be no place to hide in the Latin words of his prayer however on this pain filled night. 'Where are the words of comfort and hope he is expected to give the family of this little boy?' he thought. He prayed a silent prayer, 'God be with me and with those who gather in the pain of this night. Help me to know what words to say.' He turned and left the dim light of the room.

Mary and Frank soon followed and thanked the Father for blessing their son. "Mary," Father began, "If your son lives, if he ever awakens he will never be the same. He may not be able to walk or talk, and most likely have to be fed as he may be unable to lift a spoon to his mouth. Let God take him to Himself."

Father watched as the tears welled in Mary's eyes. He was witness to a woman, strong but tender, a heart broken but somehow comforted with a deep faith he barely knew. He thought of Jesus' mother Mary as she watched her son suffer. Such was the power of her presence in this moment of pain. As he stood there the silence of the moment grew louder and screamed back at him. Suddenly in shock he thought of Saint Peter's pain so many hundreds of years before, the shame and the utter terror of his lack of faith as he denied that he knew Jesus. Father Rivers was deeply troubled by what he had just said. 'Where in God's name is my faith?' he wondered. 'It was the wrong thing for him to have said to Mary of her son. Those words were not the words of a healer of the soul. What little faith he had. Perhaps, he really was overlooking the chance for the miracle of physical healing.' He looked at his hands and for the moment did not dare to lay them again upon the boy so shaken was his faith.

'Had he seen too much in the years of ministry to hold out much hope for a miracle here?' There had been a few times that he'd been witness to what he might call a miracle of healing. He could count them on one hand though. "God forgive me," he whispered to himself in the comfort of the Latin. Looking again and seeing Mary's grief and sorrow he gently spoke, "I'm so sorry Mary. Let us gather for a while and pray." The day had now turned to night. Candles were lit while family and friends gathered again in and around the room to pray. Father led in the Latin, the sounds and rhythm of prayers not understood by most who gathered but familiar and comforting just the same. The hearts and voices of all present called out to God in prayer imploring; pleading for healing, forgiveness, mercy and goodness to a God they knew each in their own way.

Father Rivers, comforted in prayer, took courage and again signed Francis with the Sign of the Cross on his forehead.

Ralph was asleep in his room. As the prayer vigil for Francis continued Barb, Cele, Lawrence and Ben sat quietly nearby. It had been a very long day. Ben began to nod off and Cele laid his head on her lap. Cele wondered at how different this afternoon and evening had been from any she had as yet experienced. As she looked at all who were present she thought of the dancing and parties with family and friends that she enjoyed. Somehow she could not understand the fullness of the pain and all that had happened this day.

Ma made her way to the doorway between the kitchen and living room near where the children sat. She leaned on the door post. "It's late, to bed with you now" she said. There was no protest, indeed Barb felt exhausted and ready for bed. Barb took Ben's hand and raised his head from his sister Cele's lap and helped his sleepy body up the stairs. Cele and Lawrence followed close behind. Lawrence whispered, "Good night little brother," as he ascended the stairs.

The three oldest knelt down and said their prayers. Each in their own way prayed for Francis and wondered about what had happened on this bright blue October day. Barb and Cele lay awake in their bed for quite some time. Without Francis the straw tick mat they slept on seemed so much bigger. They soon fell asleep.

As friends and family continued their vigil, Francis' breathing through the evening hours had gradually become labored. Then quite suddenly opening his mouth and gasping for air he suddenly fell utterly still and silent. Francis died that October night surrounded by the love of family and friends.

A Sad Farewell

Barb awoke to morning light streaming through the bedroom window. She watched as the tiny particles of dust danced in the streams of light. Then she saw them, the flowers she had placed in the vase on the stand by the bed. And the thought of Francis took over her thoughts.

She got down on her knees and began her morning prayer. As she recited her prayers she could not help but hear the muffled sounds in the kitchen below. Her prayer again drifted into thoughts of her brother. 'Was he still sleeping? Had he died? If he did, was he in heaven this morning? Was the sun shining bright there too? Or maybe he was still on his way. Or did she dare to hope that somehow he was better and might soon be able to run and play again. Never again would she tease him or be the slightest bit unkind,' she vowed. Prayer and thought were one and the same. The smell of bacon frying broke free for the moment thoughts of her brother. Quickly she made the Sign of the Cross and jostled her sister Cele and her brothers out of their slumber. Then she headed for the door to see her brother.

Just then Ma entered the room. Barb looked at her ma. She stood silent for a moment, without a word and Barb knew what had happened in the night while she slept. Ma stood quietly as the kids rose from their beds her eyes moistened by tears, she gazed upon her children. She said simply in a soft unwavering voice, "Kids, Francis died during the night." They looked at their mother with looks of confusion and disbelief at what she had said. For a moment they looked at one another and looking again at Ma's face searched for clues as to what they might say or what they might do. Tears began to flow and they gathered around their ma hoping for some kind of comfort for themselves and for their ma. "There is breakfast for you now" she said, and one by one they descended the stair into the kitchen.

Barb looked through the door into the living room and saw the door to Ma and Dad's room was closed. It was a sad morning. The bacon and buns Barb loved seemed to have lost their flavor. The deliciousness of this Saturday morning breakfast seemed to have died with her brother.

This day there were chores to do and meals to fix but they were done out of love by others. The day was far from ordinary as all day long friends and family came and went bringing with them food and offers to help in whatever ways they could. Sometime late in the day a coffin, in which Francis would be laid, was carried into the house by friends and family. Carefully they placed it on a stand that was set against a wall in the living room. Flowers filled the room and candles in fancy candelabras, were placed by friends and family. People came and went through the afternoon and into the evening.

Dad and Ma welcomed and greeted them all. Never before it seemed had there been so many family and friends gathered together at one time. Young people, both cousins and neighborhood friends, gathered in the yard, played games and visited about all that had happened. The adults gathered and visited inside and outside the house as well. Cars and buggies lined the driveways and overflowed into both yard and field.

The sun set behind dark gathering clouds. One by one family and friends said their good-byes. Uncle Pete and Uncle Mike remained to stand wake through the night with the body of their young nephew Francis.

Barb kneeling on the floor, arms on the sill, watched the storm out of the upstairs bedroom window where Ma sat in the rocking chair holding her baby close. Val nursed contentedly as Ma slowly rocked back and forth. The wood creaked in a rhythmic and steady measure.

Stars had shown on the night of Francis's death and on this night the countryside lit up with lightning for long moments as numerous strikes cascaded among the storm clouds. The sound of thunder rumbled and echoed through hills and valley. And there she was, Fanny, white against the dark of the sky. In full gallop she came, out from the trees into the clearing of the pasture. As she neared the fenced edge of the pasture she would lift her head and with a loud whinny turn, again with mane and tail flowing, head back into the trees at full gallop. Barb mesmerized by the scene that unfolded, watched as time and again Fanny continued her ritual. It was as though Fanny somehow knew and she too shared in the anguish and pain of the day gone by.

Each time Fanny disappeared into the trees the events of the day ran through Barb's head like a picture show of light flashing an image on the screen of a theatre. She thought of all who had lent a hand to help her ma and dad in their grief and all the cousins who came and somehow were able to make the day at times almost fun. She felt pangs of guilt for having been able to laugh if only for a while. She wondered about how she should feel at the death of her brother. She certainly sensed the sadness of all that had happened.

As Barb had eaten her breakfast this morning, the boiler sat on the stove as if it were a wash day. Ma brought sheets on which Francis had laid, stained with blood and began to wash them. She watched as the water in the washtub darkened. Barb did not see the tears of her ma mix with water, as Ma did not raise her eyes from her work. Barb knew why her ma washed the sheets. Those were the only sheets Ma had and there wasn't money to buy new ones. She had heard too often the voices of Ma and Dad as conversation escalated in frustration for lack of money and the drudgery of farm life.

A flash and loud clap of thunder rattled the window and startled Barb. She turned to see her ma holding Val now asleep in her arms. "It's getting late Barb. It's been a long day. Better be getting to bed now," Ma said. Barb turned for a moment to see only the darkness of the night. A gentle rain was falling now and rivulets of raindrops trickled down the panes of glass. She arose and made her way to bed.

Cele was already asleep and Barb lay down upon the bed. She had often been annoyed that her brother slept with her and Cele in the same straw tick bed. And now, how she missed him. Soon she drifted off and the much needed sleep enfolded her.

Sunday came and again there were friends and family. Offers to help and rides to Sunday Mass were provided. Later in the afternoon again the driveways and edges of the fields filled with cars. The killing frost of fall had not yet arrived and the color and beauty of flower bouquets from gardens of the surrounding countryside filled the house with the sweet scent of life. Strangely, for a brief moment, it somehow seemed almost normal now.

Friends and neighbors came and went throughout the afternoon and into the evening. Dad and Ma welcomed them all, comforted by their words and expressions of sympathy. A final wake service was held that Sunday evening.

Morning came and on the chill Monday morning of October 12, 1931 Francis was laid to rest in a new cemetery on the north hill overlooking the city of Glenwood. Several hundred family and friends came to honor the little chap they had loved so much.

Later that week the Thursday, October 15, 1931 Glenwood paper carried a short article on its upper left front page with the heading "Dies Of Injuries From Accident."

Ma, taking a moment, sat down and read the article. Dad, standing behind the kitchen chair where she sat glanced down at the article too.

The article ended with the following paragraphs.

> *"Seldom is an entire community so heart stricken as was occasioned by the tragic death of this little chap whom everyone, that knew him, loved and admired. Hundreds of neighbors, relatives and friends attended the last sad rites on Monday.*

Pallbearers were Kenneth Salmon, Robert Jackelen, Wm. Jackelen, Frank Casselius, Earl Casselius, and Walter Casselius.

Funeral services were held at 9 o'clock at the house, and at 10 o'clock ~ from St. John's Catholic Church. Rev. Fr. P. G. Rivers officiated. Internment was made in St. John's Catholic Cemetery.

Francis Jackelen leaves to mourn his untimely demise, his parents, Mr. and Mrs. Frank Jackelen; four brothers, Lawrence, Ralph, Bernard and Valy; and two sisters, Celia and Barbara."

Dad placed his hand gently on Ma's shoulder. Not a word was said. Dad turned and walked to the door. Removing his coat from the coat hook he put it on. Taking his hat from a coat pocket he opened the door and closing it behind him, walked to the barn. As Dad walked alone he noticed the many marks from the wheels of dozens of cars and buggies and the many footsteps imprinted upon the earth.

Ma sat for some time staring at the paper on the table in front of her. Carefully folding the paper she got up from her chair. She walked to the bedroom. Entering the room Ma glanced for a moment at the table next to the bedside on which sat the bottle of Holy Water. Removing it from the table she opened the closet door and put it and the paper in her place of safekeeping. Closing the closet door she walked from the bedroom and went about the housework.

Epilogue

I began the story of "Francis, The Uncle I Never Knew" in the winter of 2001 and finished it later that spring. The story ended with the line - *Closing the closet door she walked from the bedroom and went about the housework.*

Although the story's ending indicates life for the Jack-elen family carried on it would be easy to surmise there would be little redemption to the story. In some ways that was true as I reflected on some of the stories told by my mother, uncles and others. But in the end it is a story of a love that never ends.

There were difficult times to be sure and there were also stories of happier times. During the years that followed the death of Francis the Depression continued on for nearly a decade. During this time, unable to keep up payments, the farm went back to the bank. Many families in those years suffered the loss of all that they had worked for. The family moved to another farm where they lived and worked for a number of years. World War II had begun and America changed in many ways.

The children grew. Barb and Cele moved to the Chicago area as young women and worked with several aunts who were Franciscan Sisters of the Sacred Heart. *The Sisters min-*

istered and cared for the sick and dying at hospitals in and around the Chicago area. Cele married while in Chicago and remained there with her husband Al. Illinois was where they would live and raise their family, a boy and a girl. Lawrence, Ralph and Ben found work on local area farms. Ralph, Ben and Val, now all young men, eventually enlisted in the Army as did many of their cousins and friends. Lenny Jackelen, a cousin of my mother's, died in the Battle of Normandy and is buried in the military cemetery in Normandy, France.

Sometime later Frank and Mary's children bought a farm for their folks where they would be able to live out their retirement years without the burden of renting a place to live. Eventually all the children married, except for Ben who continued to live at home with his parents.

And so the epilogue now fast forwards...

An old violin sat in an upstairs closet room just ahead and to the right of the stair landing. Three of the four strings still in place, the E string broken, still attached to its peg curled around hanging loose. The bow lay on the floor beside it broken, horse hairs still attached. Every once in a while I would visit the old violin. I would examine the grain of the wood, its finish, the scratches and the scars. I would peer through the narrow slots into its hollow body. I'd pluck on the strings trying to make sense of how this instrument of music worked. Later, I asked mom about the violin in the room and was told it was grandpa's violin and he hadn't played it in years.

Now as I write this epilogue, I wonder. Had Francis listened to the music of this instrument that I had held in my hand when he was a young boy?

It was always fun to visit my grandparents and the farm. There were lots to do for city kids. We played in the many sheds, and sometimes climbed on the lower branches of the white pines. We did not climb the pines very often as our hands and jeans would get smeared with the pine pitch weeping from the branches. Besides, the numerous apple trees of the orchard were much easier to climb and there was no oozing sap to deal with.

Often, uncles, aunts, cousins and other friends or relatives arrived for a visit. Sometimes Mike and Lizzie, or Margaret and Josie. It was indeed a gathering place.

One of the jobs mom gave to us when visiting the farm in early to mid July, was to accompany her into the woods and help with the picking of wild raspberries, both red as well as black, my favorite. Margaret and Josie, grandpa's sisters, sometimes accompanied us on our excursions. A couple of holes would be punched, using a hammer and nail, into the sides of coffee cans. Fencing wire would be threaded through the holes and the ends then twisted. Our pants belt or twine would be passed through the wire handle and buckled or tied. We would now have both hands free for the picking of berries. The job usually lasted until the pails were full.

The menfolk visiting the farm usually gathered at some point, leaning on a car or two, or sat on the tailgate of a pickup parked in the drive, chewing their snoose or smoking and drinking their beer. They conversed and shared the ordinary stuff of their days. Cars were often a subject for discussion, makes, models, and the size of engines and tires and on and on. Another subject was where and who had moved and was now living on what place. It seemed as though it was a memory game in progress. And once in a while they would visit about the crops, prices and the business of farming, most especially if things were not going well.

More times than not I would hang around for a while and just listen. As a courtesy I suppose, or maybe not, grandpa or an uncle would offer me a pinch of snuff from time to time. I never took them up on it and probably because of the "first time I ever tried snuff..."stories I had heard. To this day I have never tried the stuff. I would however take a sip of beer when it was offered. Since I was a young kid I always liked the taste. Sips are all I ever got, and that was probably a good thing.

At this time of their lives my grandparents had no car, tractor, horses or other form of transportation. They relied on their now adult children and Ben, who lived with them much of the time, as well as neighbors and others to take them to town for the things they might need. There was almost always someone to take them to church on Sundays.

Life as I experienced it at the farm was rather ordinary. Sometimes Grandpa would be away for a day or so, and when he wasn't around I didn't much notice. Once in a while as we played about the farm we would discover an empty bottle or two. We usually brought them to the house and not much was ever said, except a comment or two from my mother about how she wished Dad would quit his drinking. My mom hated drinking period. Everyone knew it.

One summer day some years later, Grandma remained in her upstairs bedroom. We questioned mom why Grandma hadn't come down and were told she was not feeling well. Later that afternoon a car turned into the drive and parked. A man in a suit got out with a black bag in his hand walked up to the door and was immediately invited in. We went to the house and asked Mom about him. "He's Grandma's doctor and is checking on her to see that she is alright. Grandma's not feeling well," was all she said. So back outside we went and continued our play.

Later we found out that Grandma had suffered a heart attack, though we had no concept of what that was. We were told that she would be alright in a few days and that she would have to take it easy for a while.

Late that same fall, Grandpa and Grandma moved from the farm into a used trailer home that my uncles and mom had purchased for them. The trailer had been moved and set near the house of my Uncle Lawrence and Aunt Betty's farm. Their farm was a dairy farm on two hundred twenty acres of land near Clear Lake, Wisconsin, about sixteen miles from my grandparent's farm. Lawrence and Betty had three children, Mike, Susie and Mary Beth.

And so the trailer was now the new home of my grandparents. I was happy that Grandma and Grandpa were now living on Uncle Lawrence and Aunt Betty's farm for it was another favorite place of mine. For a couple of years my brother Greg and I would each have our own week for a summer stay on the farm and how we both enjoyed our weeks with our cousins.

My mother had decided that we would stay one at a time as she figured it would be easier for Aunt Betty, though I don't believe it mattered much to my aunt. For our cousins perhaps it allowed for an additional week of company, just a little different than the same old routine. However in those summers, the routine was there was no routine. There were, at the time, a number of other cousins who spent time at uncle and aunt's farm as well. Two of Uncle Val and Aunt Bev's boys, Donny and Tommy were regulars and then there was Aunt Betty's twin sister Jane, her husband, Chester and their three children, Art, Kitzie and Mark. And so the size of my Uncle Lawrence and Aunt Betty's household fluctuated throughout the summer months. Chester was Uncle Lawrence's partner in the farm work and his right hand man.

In many ways life for Grandma and Grandpa was made so much easier. There was running water in the trailer, no pails to be filled with water from the pump-house and then carried into the house for its use. There was even a flush toilet. Wash days for Grandma were so much easier. No wood fires to stoke or boiler on the stove on wash days and all the lifting and work the process demanded. No wringer washer. No more outhouse. And the list goes on.

My Aunt and Grandmother often combined wash day and gave assistance to one another. One day, they were washing clothes and hanging them outside to dry in the summer breeze. My cousin Mike, his cousin Art and I were in a hay field just to the north of the house. We were baling hay and the knotter on the baler kept miss-tying nearly every bale, or so it seemed. We'd go for a short distance, stop, remove one of many strings from miss tied bales which were draped about the tension spring and tie a loop on one end. Next we'd loop the broken string on both ends of the bale, push the bale together and using the string with the loop, thread the string through the loops and tie it as tight as we could. Sometimes, there was no saving the bale and we would carry loose hay in armfuls and scatter it down the windrow of hay still to be baled. It was a tedious, frustratingly ridiculous afternoon. After some choice words and expletives, and there were quite a few said as I recall, the harvest of hay on that field was finished.

Later as we gathered for supper my Aunt made casual mention of what Grandma had said to her as she came in from hanging the clothes. We already knew what was coming. "The boys must be having a difficult time in the field today," she said. The three of us looked at one another with a kind of "oops." The breeze had been from the north that day. It amazes me how God and grandmas work together.

Grandpa helped with the morning and evening chores during the school year feeding the cows, calves and scraping barn-walks, doing whatever jobs needed doing. Grandpa and Uncle Lawrence were never much for conversation and I'm not sure there was ever much said as chores were done.

Grandpa, still consumed with his need for a drink, continued his binges and one day found himself blacklisted in the bars and liquor establishments around Clear Lake.

Grandpa came home from town that day, upset with the blacklisting and said to his daughter-in-law Betty, "I'd like to know who the SOB was that put me on the blacklist." Betty, looked him in the eye and replied, "You're looking at her." Grandpa, stupefied for a moment, turned and just walked away. My aunt, all five feet two of her was a fearless woman.

Grandpa's drinking binges at least for a while were not as frequent and severe and he was better behaved. Somehow though, he managed to continue the drinking, sometimes hitching a ride to another town or finding other ways to continue his drinking, though probably not near as frequently as he would have liked.

Sometimes my cousin Mike would get jabbed with words from kids on the school bus referencing Frank. Mike, quick and stern in his reply would put a quick end to their remarks. "Look, why don't you just shut up! He is my grandpa! Have some respect." I imagine Susie and Mary may have suffered the same.

The years passed by. I graduated from Hill High School in St. Paul, Minnesota in the spring of 1968. With money I had received from family and friends for my accomplishment, I bought a five speed Schwinn Collegiate model bicycle in early June. A couple of weeks later, early on a Sunday morning having packed up some clothes, toiletries and whatever I figured I would need for a week's stay, began a sixty mile trip on my bike to my Uncle and Aunt's farm. I stayed for the week and rode back with my family the following Sunday.

I worked that July and August in the factory where my father worked and began college in the fall of 1968. As family we continued to visit grandma and grandpa, our uncle, aunt and cousins as often as we could. Mostly the times and the visits were quite ordinary.

It was March 5th 1969 on a Saturday evening and Grandpa and Grandma had finished cleaning up after supper. Vatican II changes in the Catholic Church were in progress. Mass was now all in English. The Sunday Mass could now be said on the Saturday afternoon or evening preceding the Sunday. That became for my grandparents a preferred time to attend Sunday Mass. On this evening for some reason they were not able to go. The Sign of Peace had just recently been implemented into the Liturgy of the Mass at St. John's in Clear Lake. Grandma decided to go to bed a bit earlier than was usual on this evening and so she and Grandpa shook hands as an offering of God's Peace for one another. Wishing one another a good night, Grandma went off to bed.

Frank called to Mary a couple of times; receiving no response from her, he entered her bedroom about 6:00am that Sunday morning. Sometime early in the morning hours of March 6th, 1969, Grandma Mary died in her sleep. She was 80 years old

I awoke that morning to my mother's weeping.

A few days later we attended the wake and the Funeral Mass for Mary, a wife of 52 years, a mother of seven children and twenty-six grandchildren. Her burial service was held some two months later in May, as the ground was frozen at the time of her death. My mother later mentioned to me how difficult the day of burial was for her.

On the morning Grandma Mary died, one of Grandma Mary's two surviving sisters or nieces, Franciscan Sisters of the Sacred Heart, relayed the following story to a member of the family. In Chapel, while at prayer in the early morning around the time of Mary Jackelen's death, one of the Sisters witnessed a bright light moving through the chapel.

As I write this epilogue, all of the relatives of my mother's generation are deceased, but for Uncle Val. I recall the story from my memory of a time in the days following Mary's death. I have contacted others to confirm the event; however, no one I have contacted in regard to the light in the chapel could verify the conversation or had heard the story.

Grandpa continued to live in the trailer alone helping Lawrence with the daily chores.

One summer afternoon we were sitting by the side of the barn. We had come down from the heat of the mow and were relaxing for a while as we awaited the next wagon load of hay. I looked up the drive and Grandpa was making his way down the drive carrying a paper bag. As Grandpa neared the place where we were sitting one-by-one we acknowledged him with a "Hi Grandpa." Someone asked, "What's in the bag?" "Would anyone like to try some dandelion wine?" he asked. We all looked about at one another. Always the adventurer I said, "I'll try some." Grandpa pulled the bottle out of the bag, and poured a juice glass half full. I took it and noticed the bouquet and the lightness of color. I took a sip, and then another... "Not bad Grandpa." I said. The others tried a few sips as well that day and we all agreed it was some OK wine. We visited with Grandpa for a while and he then made his way up the drive to his trailer house. Soon we were back at it with another load of hay to be stacked in the mow.

From time to time our family would visit Grandpa and my Uncle, Aunt and cousins at the farm. I was still in college and didn't get away nearly as much as I would have liked. When I could, I visited the farm as it was for me a favorite place to spend time. From time to time I visited with Grandpa however I don't recall much of anything out of the ordinary in our conversations. Time passed.

One day in the fall of 1973, Uncle Ralph brought Grandpa to our house in St. Paul to stay with us for a few days. Grandpa had an appointment to see a doctor at the VA Hospital in Minneapolis on the following day. After a number of doctor visit's Grandpa was hospitalized and after a stay of a couple of weeks it was found he had terminal cancer.

Through tests they determined there was not much medically that could be done for him.

Sometime in December, the Little Sisters of the Poor Convent and Care Center, located in St. Paul, about four miles from where we lived, took Grandpa in. There he received the care he needed for the remainder of his life.

My cousin Don married in February of 1974. The afternoon of the wedding dance I went to pick Grandpa up at the Sister's Care Center. We seated Grandpa in the passenger seat of my slightly used, newly purchased 1973 purple Gremlin; now there is a vision of an artist's car. I loaded his wheelchair into the hatchback and off we went to the dance. Grandpa was able to dance with the bride, Pam, and several other ladies that evening. Though Grandpa enjoyed dancing, because his legs were weakened by his illness, Grandpa spent most of his time in the wheelchair and listened to the music. He seemed to enjoy the evening and visited with all who took the time to stop by and say "hi."

My brother Greg and his fiancée, Darlene invited Grandpa to their upcoming June 6th wedding of that same year. Grandpa accepted the invitation and was excited by the prospect of another upcoming wedding and dance.

As the days and weeks followed it was clear Grandpa would not celebrate the wedding of another grandchild.

Grandpa Frank died on the afternoon of April 22, 1974 at the age of 79. My brother Greg and Darlene were married about six weeks later on June 6, 1974.

* * * * * * * *

Some thirty-two years later while taking down exhibits in the Dairy Building on the morning after the close of the 2006 Minnesota State Fair, I had a chance meeting with a Sister of the Little Sisters of the Poor. Sister had come to pick up food that was being donated by one of the clients I was working for on take-down day at the fair. Her name tag read, Sr. Emmanuel. 'The name is familiar,' I thought. I then said to her, "I had a grandpa that was at the Little Sisters of the Poor maybe thirty years ago." She paused but for a moment, "Was his name Frank Jackelen?" she asked. I replied, "Why, yes." I stood almost in unbelief of what she had said. She then said, "Yes, I remember Mr. Jackelen. He was a beautiful man." We visited for just a short minute or so and then the both of us continued with the business at hand.

This petit vibrant nun dressed in white, was for me, a messenger of God's love on a bright September day on the Tuesday following Labor Day, 2006.

In the writing of this epilogue I now know the ending of the story had already been written nearly six years earlier by Sister Emmanuel of the Little Sisters of the Poor.

Such a beautiful ending and new beginning to the story of my Uncle Francis and the family of my Mother, I would have never imagined; but for the divine mercy and love of God.

http://www.littlesistersofthepoorstpaul.org

THE STRENGTH OF FAMILY

It wasn't until I wrote the story of Francis that I began to perceive and understand the strength, patience, forgiveness and love needed to carry a family through. Perhaps even more so today, families are in sore need of those virtues.

I can only surmise my Mother's and her family's life experience but one thing I do know, their spirits were strong. In all the visits I had with Grandma and Grandpa I never sensed bitterness or defeat. I only remember their firm, yet gentle ways and the warmth of a kitchen filled with the aromas of so many good things; breakfasts, buttered bread, buns and a cookie jar, seldom if ever empty.

As a young man I never thought to ask Grandma or Grandpa about their life stories. I do not know that grandma ever kept a diary. If she did it would not surprise me that her thoughts for the most part were ordinary and peaceful. As I remember she had a shoe box or two with cards and clippings, mixed among some letters and photos she kept. Along with those things were a few broaches, some jewelry and a string of pearls that she wore on her wedding day. Sadly, Grandpa had his mementos too, empty bottles, hidden in so many places around the farm. I like to remember however, the old violin and a scythe, hung on a nail, on a wall in the old garage.

My Uncle Val was still at home when my grandparent's farm went back to the bank sometime late in the depression years. I asked him what he remembered about living in the rented farm house near Connersville, Wisconsin for some five years after the move from the farm. His response was something like this, "We lived on squirrel meat, rabbit, small game and whatever was grown, gotten or given us." He thought for a moment and in a poignant and reflective way added, "Dad worked hard all his life for so little or nothing."

The following couple of pages are based on stories told by my mother and a story titled "Grandpa's Orders" as told by my Uncle Ralph.

A Snowdrift and Two Horses

Frank hitched the team of two horses to a bob-sled wagon and headed to town. While on his way a snow storm blew in making travel nearly impossible. Frank, having made it to town did his business and waited. The storm subsided later that evening and Frank, quite intoxicated by then, decided to make for home. Sometime in the middle of the night Frank stumbled through the doorway, of the farmhouse half frozen and in a stupor. "Where are the horses and the sleigh?" Mary asked. "Caught in a drift down the road." He replied, collapsing into his chair. Mary knew she would have to go for the horses and it would take all the strength she had, both in body and spirit to do what she felt had to be done.

Mary dressed, put on her boots, coat and hat, opened the door and stepped into the wind and cold of a winter night. Trudging through the snow by the light of the moon she headed down the road toward town. Mary, afraid of horses, knew that if the horses froze that would be the end of the farm making a difficult existence even more so. The snow, hard packed by the driving wind and cold, carried her weight but often gave way making the going difficult. Coming over a rise she saw the horses and the sleigh in a drift ahead.

With the temperature below zero and the sleigh hopelessly buried, Mary unhitched the team and led the horses back to the farm and the warmth of the barn. The sleigh and what was on it would have to remain until later.

Dry Grass Fire

Often in the spring of the year after the snow is gone and before the spring rains and the greening, there is a time when the grasses of the previous fall are tinder dry. It was one of those springs and somehow the grass had caught fire and threatened the farmhouse. The only defense Frank and Mary had was to beat the flames down using the coats on their backs. The smoke from the fire made breathing difficult and the flames were hot. Both of them worked side by side until at long last the flames were extinguished. Exhausted and spent they sat for a while, grateful the house had not been burned to the ground.

Grandpa's Orders

Some years after the death of Francis, Ralph was riding through a field, bareback on Fanny, the work horse that had spooked years before, resulting in the death of his brother Francis. Ralph was riding on his way home after a visit with the neighbors. It was a beautiful summer day and Ralph was enjoying the ride. All of a sudden, there was Dad, going down the road. And there he was on the back of Fanny. Quickly, hanging tight to Fanny's mane he placed his body on the side of Fanny opposite the road, so as to hide. Fanny slowed and Ralph alighted onto the field. Fanny stopped. With reign in hand, Ralph now led Fanny on the walk home.

For Ralph a beautiful summer day had suddenly vanished. All he could think was, 'What is Dad going to do when he gets home. He had to have seen me.' How many times since the accident had he and his brothers been told, in no uncertain terms that, "Fanny was not to be ridden!" At the very least, if he was lucky, Dad would just yell at him when he got home and walked in the door.

For Ralph it was a long walk home. He took Fanny into the barnyard to the water tank. Ralph stood there while Fanny drank, all the time going through the scenarios that he figured were sure to come. Ralph led Fanny to her stall and went up to the house and waited. Later, Dad arrived home. He came through the door and never said a word. In all the days, weeks and years that followed, not a word.

Three Sisters And Two Nieces

My mother, as a young girl, was often ridiculed and teased about being Catholic by schoolmates and others. My mom spoke the following about Grandma more than once. It goes something like this – I don't know why there is all the fuss over religions? Catholic or Lutheran, we all belong to the same God and some day we will all go to that same God.

Grandma was one of eleven children born to Herman and Anna (Giese) Cassellius. There were seven sisters and four brothers. Certainly church played an important part in the lives of the Cassellius family. Three of Grandma's sisters joined the Convent of the Franciscan Sisters of the Sacred Heart as young women. Sister Edmunda Cassellius entered her Novitiate, May 1, 1916. Sister Irmengard Cassellius entered her Novitiate, March 19, 1923. Sister Marianna Cassellius entered her Novitiate, March 19, 1924.

The Cassellius family - Grandma Mary is in the lower right of this photo
The three Sisters in the back row left to right, Irmengard, Edmunda, Marianna

Years later two of Grandma's nieces entered the convent of the same order. Sister M. Ruth Anne (Gertrude) Jackelen entered her Novitiate October 4, 1937. Sister M. Matilda (Veronica) Jackelen entered her Novitiate, March 19, 1939. All of the Sisters lived and ministered at hospitals in Chicago and surrounding cities and villages in Illinois.

Gertrude and Veronica, Marie *(Twin sister to Gertrude)*, Loretta, Lillian, Will and James were the children of Mike and Lizzie Jackelen and lived on a farm just up the road from Frank and Mary Jackelen. Mike and Frank were brothers and Mary and Lizzie were sisters. And so the sons and the daughters of the two families were double cousins.

As a young boy I remember Mike and Lizzie Jackelen well. I remember one of our visits to their place. Mike sat in a chair

Sister Matilda   Mike Jackelen   Lizzie Jackelen   Sister Ruth Anne
           Brother to Frank Jackelen Sister to Mary Jackelen

next to the milk house near the end of the driveway. With his long ivory beard he looked like Santa Claus. I remember the buildings on the farm especially well. Though simple structures the proportions of the buildings were pleasing to the eye.

The farm house was a two story wood frame structure. Mike and Lizzie had a hand pitcher pump with a basin on their kitchen counter. How very modern I thought; water doesn't need to be carried from a pump to the house.

I do not recall knowing that Mike and Lizzie had two daughters who were Sisters. Years later however I would meet both Sister Matilda and Sister Ruth Anne as I drove my mother and her double cousins Lilly and Marie *(sisters to Matilda and Ruth Anne; Marie a twin sister to Ruth Anne)* to the Chicago area for a visit. I would also meet Sister Irmengard, sister to my grandmother on that visit as well.

We drove first to the Cardinal's Villa in Mundelein, Illinois where Sister Ruth Anne was working at the time. She greeted her sisters and my mother and was so happy that we had come to visit. She had wrapped gifts for her sisters and my mother but had nothing for me. Feeling badly that she did not have a gift for me she excused herself from the room and was soon back again with a bag in her hand. She said, "Please do not take offense, but this is all I have that seems appropriate as a gift for a young man." In the bag were several bars of "Irish Spring" soap. I smiled and gave her a hug and a "Thank you." It was a quintessential Franciscan gift indeed.

We then traveled to Joliet, Illinois to visit with Sister Matilda and Sister Irmengard. Sister Matilda gave the tour of St. Joseph's hospital and later Sister Irmengard joined us. We had a wonderful meal and visit in the hospital cafeteria. Sister Irmengard, a sister to my grandma Mary was in so many ways like the grandma of my memory. What a joy to spend time with her, to visit, to ask questions and to listen.

I do not recall having met Sr. Edmunda or Sr. Marianna. I met Sr. Irmengard in the 1980's. She was so much like Mary, my grandma as I remembered her. We visited about hospital work, cancer research, church, careers, relatives and friends. My mother and Aunt Cele as young women lived in the Chicago area working in hospitals staffed by their aunts. Sister Irmengard worked as a surgical supervisor for fifty-one years at St. Joseph Hospital in Joliet, Illinois.

A short time after Sister Matilda suffered a stroke, my mother, Marie and I again traveled to Illinois. I still remember Matilda's greeting as she lay in her hospital bed. I asked how she was feeling and she replied haltingly and with some difficulty. "Bob, I have the life of Riley." And she smiled a beautiful smile. I bent down and gave her a gentle hug. Sister Matilda, such a gift of joy to others, even in her pain.

In the struggles of life it is the love of family, both human and divine, that is there for us all when we are most in need.

Santa Claus AKA Sister M. Matilda

My thanks to Sr. Kathleen Moseley O.S.F. and The Franciscan Sisters of the Sacred Heart for the photos and information provided. Web site – http://www.fssh.net

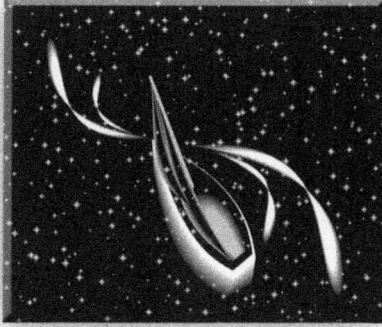

Galaxy 11 *Dreams Live On*

The winds, the energy that is life; the sails, the ship, metaphorically ours; and so we course our way through life, content in the gentle breeze and the waves of easy motion; patient in the still air and glass-like waters mirroring the sun's setting and rising; confident and strong in the merciless winds and the slamming waves of the storm. All of this is ours. It is the experience of our lives, given to each of us in different measure and at different times of our lives. And so we live one moment at a time.

Though the ships may no longer sail; the winds, the dreams of our lives carry aloft seeking out those that once sailed among us and are now at rest in the peaceful harbors of distant shores, amid distant suns in another place and time.

PEACE IN THE MORNING

Love visits at the most unexpected times and in the most unusual ways. I awoke from a dream on this morning, my being filled with a peace like I had never known before. In the dream I experienced the presence of Chester, though I could not see him. And then suddenly in the dream, peace and calm enveloped me.

Chester was a brother-in-law to my Uncle Lawrence and Aunt Betty, husband to my Aunt Betty's twin sister Jane. Most times whenever I visited my Uncle's farm Chester was there, assisting my uncle in the work of the farmer. This is what Chester chose to do for so many years. When cousin Mike took over the farm Chester continued to assist Mike with repairs, field work and whatever needed doing.

I had been to visit Chester only days before at his home in Saint Paul's Midway neighborhood. Chester was sitting in his recliner chair, ill with esophageal cancer. We shared the ordinary conversations of the day, smiling, laughing and reflecting on some of our shared moments of the past. And there was certainly a lot to draw from.

Now I lie in bed, head on my pillow. The dream was with me and I basked in the peace. I needed to share this moment. I looked over at Barb lying awake next to me. "Barb," I said, "I had the most incredible dream this morning. In the dream I was with cousin Mike. A spiral of stars like the Milky Way spun in the deepness of space in an ever so easy motion. I remember within the dream speaking to Chester, though I could not see him, and saying, "Chester, this is eternity." I went on to say, "Never have I felt so at peace, so refreshed as I do in this moment." We lay in bed and visited for a while as the clock continued forward. It was time to rise.

I got up, made coffee and sat down in my home office to check e-mails and begin the work day. A few minutes later the phone rang. I answered. "Hi Bob," came the voice I instantly recognized as Kitzie's. There was but a moment and before she could say another word I said, "I know," and in a most peaceful way added, "your dad died last night." "Did someone call you already?" she asked. "No," I said and continued, "I had this dream," and I related the dream and my experience of the peace and calm. There was a moments silence and she then replied, "Bob, are you sitting down?" I answered, "Yes." Kitzie continued, "Bob, as we spoke with Dad regarding funeral arrangements he suggested that "Herc" might say a few words at the wake and burial service." (*Herc was a nickname first given me when as a young man I struggled to lift bales of hay onto the wagons. Both Chester and Uncle Lawrence loved the name. I can still hear them; "Come on Herc, you can do it!"*) She then asked, "Bob, would you?" I replied, "Oh Kitzie, it would be an honor."

And so at the wake service I shared the scripture passage where Jesus washes the feet of his disciples; for that was what Chester did for so many years, in so many ways and for so many people. And the next morning at the cemetery burial site my brother Greg read from scripture and I shared from my heart words of comfort and peace for the families and friends who gathered at the grave. We all were blessed by the life and the love of Chester. He knew that peace and love are found in the sharing and so he shared with us all the gift of his life.

The dream remains with me through memory and every so often I reflect upon the deep peace and the calm of that wondrous morning. Living, dying, ever changing and eternal, we are the stuff of stars, of the creation. And in faith I believe death is not an end, but a new beginning.

LOVE IS A GRANDPARENT

How fortunate and thankful I am for the time spent with grandparents. I think about them from time to time. I realize now how little I really knew of them and how brief a time we spent together. How could I know the depth of their love, for the love that I knew, was that of a child.

As I think of my grandparents and my parents too, I think of the Love of God and the child that I am.

The drawing above and the following four poems were done in remembrance of my grandparents.

GRANDMA'S KITCHEN

Buns and the bread
pies in a row
all of the smells
the taste of the dough.

Strawberry jam
apple butter spread
peanut butter cookies
how well we were fed.

Flowing curtains
waving in the breeze
sunshine on tables
light through the trees

Large copper kettles
wood in the stove
heating the water
for the washing of clothes

This is grandma's kitchen.

-rb

GRANDPA'S SCYTHE

Mornings began
eggs, bacon, potatoes
all in a pan.

Screen door opens
then shuts with a slam
a hay field to cut
that is the plan.

To the wall in the shed
down with the scythe
stone wheel's turning
sparks, how they fly.

A walk to the fields
the rhythm begins
swoosh, swoosh, swoosh
swing after swing
the Timothy falls
a blanket suspended
grateful, the earth below.

Handkerchief on brow
another hot summer's day.

-rb

GRANDMA'S TIME

I stand at the door of her room
she, asleep in her chair,
her album of photos,
on the table beside her,
so many times
we have journeyed there.

"Oh, hi there,"
she says with a grin
and we look together
at the photos of the album, within.

"Would you like to go for a walk?" I ask.
Oh yes, surely I would.
So arm and arm
down the hallway we go.

We stop by the window
a golf course before us.
"Fred's working the south forty
he'll be back by noon" she says.

Oh, I'd forgotten.
These are the fields and prairies
of Nebraska, and a much earlier time.

Content and at peace,
grandma stands beside me,
Peaceful, serene,
in her distant place and time.   -rb

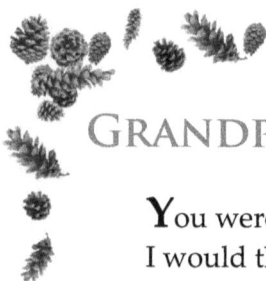

GRANDPA AND YOU

You were the grandpa
I would think about
in a worrisome sort of way.
Were you like my dad,
and my dad like you?

When you were just sixty,
you came in from the chores
as farmers daily do.
Tired, lying on the couch,
took your eternal rest.
That is all I knew of you.

Ah, but there was grandma,
the woman you loved.
The grandma who held us
my sisters, brothers and I
when we were small,
offered us tea,
scrubbed our faces,
brushed our tangled hair,
my, how we complained.

Grandma, you were our connection,
for it was, grandpa and you.

When dad turned sixty,
we kids worried a bit...
sixty-one, sixty-two...sixty-three...seventy.
-rb

$\mathcal{G}alaxy$ /2   *Sailing Through Life*

Since this book is a collection of works of art, poems, prose and other treasures based on my life experience it is as such autobiographical. There are many disparate thoughts within the works while at the same time always the reoccurring themes, of love and joy in the midst of struggle and pain, of stars and light, of mercy and forgiveness.

How, I wondered, do I connect, weave, bring to center, the variety of subjects that seemed to flow in so many directions, like the currents of on ocean. Ah, sailing! Yes, it could work and so I began the weaving, the back and forth, the stitching of needle and thread, the tacking of a sailboat on a journey through the stars.

And so the pages of this book near their end. On the following pages are photos, line drawings and writings in reference to the sailing theme and to a sailboat named Little Whee.

This line drawing was done in the late 1970's following a sail on Lake Geneva, Wisconsin with my cousin Carol's husband Rick. We launched from the public access on the southwestern shore of the lake. We began our sail mid-afternoon and sailed to Lake Geneva's eastern shore. We dined and relaxed and as the sun was setting and with no wind started our sail back under power. Clouds moved in along with the wind and a light rain began. With sails up we cut the engine and breezed along. As quickly as it had begun the rain stopped and the clouds dissipated. In the light of a full moon we made our way back sometime ahead of midnight. It was an "everything you could dream of kind of sail" but for the fact that I was with Rick. The same Rick from the story "There's Humor Somewhere" found on P. 136. What a Captain!

Little Whee was the third sailboat I designed and built. The photo above was taken on the day of the christening (June of 1982). The photo below was taken of Little Whee as she waited for summer and sailing. (A Minnesota winter and no cover - not good.)

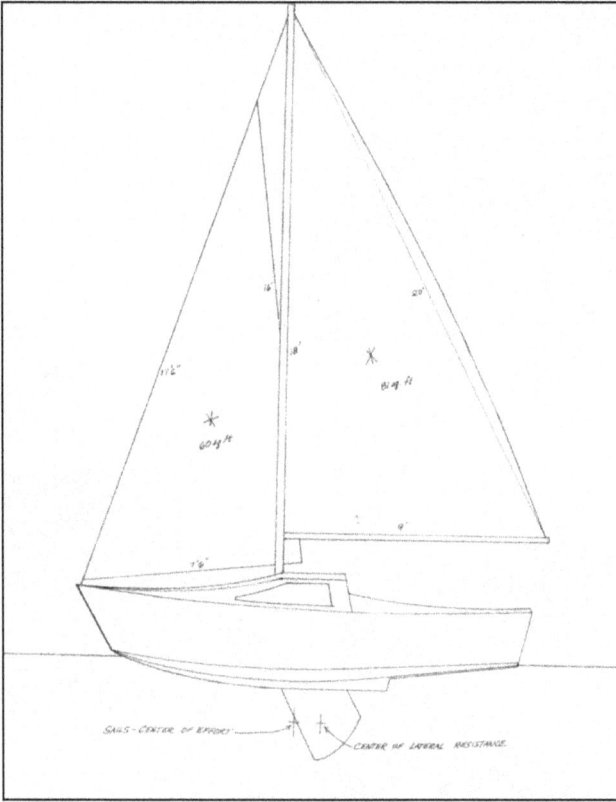

A center of effort plan shows the positioning of the mast, sails based on the lateral plane of the hull and keel below waterline, allowing for proper helm balance while under sail.

Little Whee - Photograph was taken after the cabin and deck redesign and build.

"Head in the clouds"– sketching a dream on a starboard tack. If you put yourself in the boat looking forward the sails are to your left (port side) and catching a wind blowing from the right (starboard side) The boat is moving forward with the wind on the starboard (right) side and is said to be on a starboard tack.

Beached on a sandy island on the St. Croix River near Hudson, Wisconsin. Ready for rest after a moonlight sail.

Little Whee's winter storage spot in a machine shed on my uncle's farm.

The only photo I have of the second sailboat I built. The photo was taken in the spring of 1972 the year of my graduation from the School of Associated Art. I built the boat for one of the students of the college for the cost of materials.

This photo was taken while on a overnight sail with friends in Lake Pepin on the Mississippi River. The boat is a Montgomery 17, a secure and fun boat to sail.

An Irish Prayer:
For The Sending Of Sailors

May the waves rise gentle to meet you
May the winds be ever in your favor
Making for a tack, a reach, or an easy run
May the dew of the morning
Fill the furls of your sails
May the warmth of the sun
And a quickening wind
Move your boat swiftly along
May you know peace in the storms
And hope in the doldrums of despair
And until we meet again
On that distant far off shore
May you be held in love
On the life giving oceans of God's hand

Adapted and written by the
author of this book; the prayer is
based on an old Irish prayer.
-rb

This drawing was created one summer afternoon as I sat in my car in the driveway of the farm, an odd place to do a sketch such as this. There must have been a show of "Aurora Borealis" the night before.

Barb and I were visiting my cousin Jerry, his wife Mary Kae and family in their home in Elgin Illinois. The first word I ever remember our first son David speaking was on the evening of that visit. Not yet one year of age, he spoke quite plainly the words "good night" as he went to bed. Jerry, brother to my cousin Carol, are my mother's sister Cele and Al Hoffman's children.

I close this book, simply, with a poem written by our son David, and printed with permission.

NIGHT

The sky is star filled.
Warmth fills the air and the breeze calms
All that it touches.

-db   I wrote this poem because I like nighttime in the summer.